Robinson Sadi

Flowers Culled from the Gulistan, or Rose Garden, and from the Bostan

Or Pleasure Garden of Sadi

Robinson Sadi

Flowers Culled from the Gulistan, or Rose Garden, and from the Bostan
Or Pleasure Garden of Sadi

ISBN/EAN: 9783337082789

Printed in Europe, USA, Canada, Australia, Japan

Cover: Foto ©Andreas Hilbeck / pixelio.de

More available books at **www.hansebooks.com**

FLOWERS

CULLED FROM THE

GULISTAN, OR ROSE GARDEN,

AND FROM

THE BOSTAN,

OR

PLEASURE GARDEN OF SADI,

A Persian Poet, who flourished in the 13th Century.

~~~~~~~~~~~~

"WHOSO IS WILLING TO PROFIT BY GOOD COUNSEL WILL DO WELL TO RECEIVE IT FROM THE WORDS OF SADI."

~~~~~~~~~~~~

LONDON:
PUBLISHED BY WILLIAMS & NORGATE,
HENRIETTA STREET, COVENT GARDEN;
AND BY JAMES CORNISH, MANCHESTER.

MDCCCLXXVI.

PRELIMINARY NOTICE.

Of the distinguished authors of Persia, none perhaps have enjoyed in the Eastern world a more decided and wider popularity than Sadi, and few, if indeed any, have so nearly attained that rank even in our Western world. He early won the attention of European scholars through a Latin translation of his best known work, the Gulistân, or Rose Garden, made by George Gentius, and published by him at Amsterdam, A.D. 1651, under the title of Rosarium Politicum. The fame of this celebrated production has since, but with a considerable interval of time, been extensively diffused by other translations into the principal languages of Europe: in our own by those of Gladwin, Dumoulin, Lee, Ross, and more recently an excellent one by Professor Eastwick; in German, by Nesselmann and Graf; in France, by Semelet. This celebrity has been deservedly merited by the good sense and wit and wisdom of the author, by his knowledge of the world and human nature, by his religious feeling and high moral tone, and by the general clearness and simplicity of his style ; in which last particular he stands, comparatively speaking, in remarkable contrast to the ordinary redundancy of expression, and exaggeration of sentiment and figure, in Persian composition.

Shaikh-Muslah-ud-Din Sadi was born at Shiráz, the capital of Persia, or rather of the province of Fars, which might not be improperly entitled the Persian Athens, in the closing years of the twelfth century : a period in which Europe was slowly emerging from mediæval darkness. He was patronized by the Atabeg Saad-ben-Zingi, the then Ruler of Fars, at whose Court his father is said to have held some office. He appears to have been educated, in part at least, in the Nizamian College at Baghdad, and to have been a pupil of the Shaikh Abdul Kadar Gilani, who instructed him in theology and the principles of the Sufi sect, and with whom he made his first Pilgrimage to Mecca; which he is said to have repeated in his after-life fourteen times. He was, as we gather from notices in his works, in the course of it a great traveller in distant countries, and is said to have assisted in the Holy Wars against the Infidels in Asia Minor and in India :—

" I have wandered through various quarters of the world,
And spent my days conversing with every one I met :
In every corner I found something to profit me ;
From every sheaf I gathered an ear."

On one occasion, he tells us himself, that whilst he
had withdrawn into the desert near Jerusalem to
perform his religious exercises, he was made captive
by the Franks, who sent him to work with some Jews
in digging the trenches at Tripoli. Here he was
recognized by an acquaintance whom he had known
at Aleppo, and who, pitying his sad condition,
redeemed him with ten dinars, took him home with
him, and subsequently married him to his daughter,
giving him a portion of one hundred dinars. This
marriage did not prove a happy one. Her disposition,
he says, was ill-tempered and abusive, so that it quite
destroyed his comfort. One day tauntingly she
exclaimed, " Art not thou the man whom my father
bought for ten dinars?" " Yes," he replied, " and
sold to thee for a hundred !"

Sadi married a second time at Sanâa, the capital of
Yemen. We may hope that his second nuptials were
crowned with more felicity than his first appears to
have been. In the Bostân is found an affecting
passage, in which he deplores the death of his son in
terms of the most poignant anguish. The events of
Sadi's life recorded by his biographers are but few,

and those few rest probably on little authority. Perhaps the Poet himself is his own best and most authentic recorder of his acts and opinions. For the attentive reader of his works will be able to form a very fair estimate of what he did, and what he thought, and what he was, and will find presented to his view in them a lively and interesting portraiture of an intelligent, wise, and estimable man. If the story be true, that when the Minister of Hulaku Khan sent him a present of 50,000 dinars he expended them on a house of entertainment for travellers, he practised the generosity which he so often and so well inculcates in his precepts.

If to the period of his childhood and youth and the time passed in the Nizamian College in his education and theological studies we add the thirty years which he is reported to have consumed in his travels and the various adventures of his wandering life, Sadi must have been already of more than mature age, when, as he is said to have done, he returned to his native city Shiráz, where he spent the remainder of his days in retirement, in religious contemplation, in receiving the friends and strangers, whom his great fame drew around him or attracted to visit him, and probably in the composition of his various works, of which Rose in his life enumerates twenty-two, and

Sir Gore Ouseley in his Biographical Notices of the Persian Poets gives a list with their titles of twenty-four, and which he probably would hardly have had the leisure to execute on his journeys. His life appears to have been prolonged to extreme old age, though we may be excused from accepting Daulet Shah's his biographer's assertion that it was extended to one hundred and two years. He was buried near Shirâz, where his tomb was seen by Kaempfer in 1683, who describes it at that time as almost a ruin; by Franklin in 1786-7, who says that unless repaired it must soon fall entirely to decay; and again by Sir Gore Ouseley in 1811, who, from the reverence in which he held Sadi, wished himself to do something to save it from destruction. But the Governor of Fars, "too proud," he says, " to accede to my wishes, and too avaricious to be at the expense himself, would not allow me to carry my intentions into execution, but promised himself to put it into as fine a state of repair as the Vakil Kerim Khan had done the tomb of Hafiz. But he has not fulfilled his promise, and "it is to be feared and lamented that ere long not a stone will tell where the once brightest ornament of Persia —the matchless possessor of piety, genius, and learning—was entombed."

In the picture which Franklin saw of him near the

tomb, he is represented as wearing "the khirkah"—
the long blue gown of a Derwish, with a staff in his
hand.

———

Sadi, as intimated above, was not only a voluminous
writer, but on a variety of subjects. But his fame,
which has endured in the East with apparently
undiminished lustre for upwards of six centuries,
rests especially on two works — his Gulistân,
or Rose Garden, and his Bostân, which may be
rendered most appropriately perhaps in English by
Pleasure Garden. The last, which is commonly
regarded as the later work, was really the earlier.
The Gulistân, the best known by English readers,
through several translations, as noted before, is a
collection of short stories, anecdotes, founded on his
own experience, or that of others, and general
observations on life, character, and manners, written
partly in prose and partly in verse; the narrative
portions being commonly in prose, and the more
weighty maxims and dignified sentiments and more
poetical descriptions in verse, in rhymed couplets or
other measures. Of the English translations, the
only one which preserves the *Form* of the original is
that of Professor Eastwick, published by Stephen

Austin, of Hertford, in 1850, beautifully printed, and elegantly embellished in the Persian style. Of the Bostân, the translator knows no complete version except the German one of Graf, of which there is an edition published at Jena, in two small volumes, in 1850; nor, indeed, of any translations from it into English, excepting of very few and scattered passages. So far as he is aware, the following specimens present a much more considerable portion of it than can be found elsewhere, and therefore the following little volume may be not unacceptable to the mere English reader who may desire to form a somewhat larger acquaintance with Sadi's writings. It may be proper to mention that the greater part has appeared before in a little volume of miscellaneous translations from various Persian authors, entitled "Flowers culled from Persian Gardens," from which, being now quite out of print, those which were from Sadi are here reprinted separately, arranged in a more orderly manner, and with not, it is hoped, unimportant or uninteresting additional specimens.

S. R.

Wilmslow, 1876.

To this little volume the Translator has been tempted to append two or three specimens of another distinguished Persian author who, like Sadi, wrote on moral and religious subjects, and belongs to the same age of Persian literature. This is the celebrated Jelal-ud-din, the writer of a long and remarkable poem on "Divine Love and the Sufi Philosophy," strongly imbued with that mystic spirituality to which that nation is strongly inclined, and which forms so characteristic a feature in their compositions, and often lends them a peculiar charm. He was born at Balkh, in the very last years of the twelfth century, and was therefore, in the strictest sense, the actual contemporary of Sadi himself.

He was of an illustrious family, his grandmother, according to the account given in Sir Gore Ouseley's Notices of Persian Poets, being a daughter of a King of the Kharismian dynasty, and his mother a daughter of a King of Khorasan; and his father tracing up his ancestry to the Commander of the Faithful, the Kalif Abubekr. He is said to have enjoyed, through his sanctity and learning, the respect and affection of the inhabitants of Balkh to such a degree as to excite the jealousy of the Sultan Mohammed Kharizm Shah, who held his Court in that city, and that in consequence of the annoyances he received on that account, he finally abandoned his native place, resolved never to return to it, taking with him his family and many of his disciples.

He first directed his steps to Mecca, and after visiting the Hejâz and the tombs of the saints in Syria, and wandering about for several years, arrived at Constantinople, and finally fixed his residence at Koniah, the ancient Iconium, in Syria; from which circumstance he probably derives his surname of Rûmi, Rûmi meaning very generally Syria.

By his father's will, and with the general approval of those who had adopted Sufi doctrines, Jelal-ud-Din Rûmi became the head and spiritual guide to the professors of Sufi-ism, and succeeded to the title of Sultan ul Ulema (*Ruler of the Learned*); and, after his accession to the Chair, four hundred additional students, it is said, joined the College, and sought the benefit of his instructions. It is not improbable that with his mind directed to such contemplations and studies, it was here that he composed, or at least finished, his great Poem.

TABLE OF CONTENTS.

Part I.

List of Specimens by the same Translator at the end.

PART I.

~~~~~~~~~~

FLOWERS FROM THE GULISTAN, OR ROSE-GARDEN.

~~~~~~~~~~

TO WHAT USE WILT THOU APPLY A TRAY OF ROSES?
PLUCK THOU RATHER A LEAF OUT OF MY GARDEN.
THE ROSE MAY CONTINUE TO BLOOM FIVE OR SIX DAYS;
BUT MY ROSE-GARDEN IS FRAGRANT FOR EVER.

Sadi.

FLOWERS FROM THE GULISTAN, OR ROSE-GARDEN OF SADI.

FROM THE INTRODUCTION.

O, bounteous Lord, who from thine hidden treasury providest sustenance for the pagan and the infidel, how canst Thou exclude Thy friends from Thy presence! Thou who thus regardest even thine enemies.

Behold the generosity and kindness of the All-powerful One! His servant has committed a fault, and He it is who is ashamed for him.

Cloud, and wind, sun, moon, and sky are all busy to bring bread to thine hand: eat it not in neglect-fulness.

All for Thy sake are in motion and obedient : it is
not the rule of justice that thou only shouldst be
disobedient.

O Thou great beyond imagination, or measure, or
thought, or conjecture; beyond all that has been
spoken, or heard, or read, the assembly is concluded;
we have arrived at the term of life, and we are still
at the commencement only of our acknowledgment
of Thine attributes.

One day in the bath a friend put into my hand a
piece of perfumed clay (*used by the Persians as soap*).
I said to it, " Art thou musk or ambergris ? for I am
charmed with thy delicious smell !"

It replied, " I was a piece of worthless clay, but I
sat for some time in the company of the rose.

The excellence of my companion was imparted
to me : otherwise I should still have been the clay
that I was."

Shame on the man who departeth and hath not
finished his work !

Who, when the drum soundeth for departure, hath
not made up his burthen.

Who, on the morning of his journey, is still in-
dulging in sweet sleep;

And is detaining him who hath to journey on foot.

Since die thou must, whether good or bad, happy
art thou if thou bearest off the ball of goodness!
Send thyself provisions for thy solace before thee to
the tomb; send them before thee, for no one will
bring them after thee.

———

Whoever comes hither has begun a new building,
and then has given over the tenement to another.
And that other has altered it in like manner according
to his own wishes; so that no one has ever brought
the building to its completion.

———

Life is snow under the sun of July: but a little
remains, and will the merchant still be slothful? O
thou, who hast gone empty-handed to the market, I
fear thou wilt not bring back a full napkin!

———

O man of intelligence, what is the tongue in thy
mouth but the key which opens the door of the wise
man's treasure!—If the door is kept locked, what
knows any one whether he sells jewels, or is a mere

pedlar ? Two things are a sign of a weak understanding: to keep your lips closed at the time for
speaking, and to speak at the time for silence.

A company of Indian sages were conversing about
the qualities of Bezerchemher, and declared that they
knew in him but one fault: that he was slow of
speech. Bezerchemher overheard them, and said,
" To think well what I shall say is better than to be
ashamed of what I have said." Reflect, and then utter
your words; and when you have said enough, stop
before they say,—" Enough!" Man is in speech
better than the brutes: but if you speak not justly,
the brutes are better than you."

They asked Solomon, the wise, from whom he
learnt wisdom. He answered, from the blind; for
till they have tried the ground, they plant not the
foot.

FROM THE FIRST CHAPTER, ON THE QUALITIES OF KINGS.

Upon the portico of the. Court of Feridun was written :—

"The world, O my brother, abideth with no one;

Fix thine heart on Him who created it: that is enough.

Place not reliance or trust in the sovereignty of Fortune, for many a one, like thyself, she hath nurtured and destroyed.

When the pure soul is on the point of departing, what mattereth it whether it be on a throne or on the bare ground."—*Ch. I.* 1.

The name of Nushirvan still liveth, renowned for his goodness,

Though a long time hath passed since Nushirvan hath ceased to live.

Practice goodness thou,—whoever thou art—and turn thy life to profit,

Before a cry is raised :—such a one is no more.— *Ch. I.* 2.

The tree which has only just now been planted, the strength of a man may tear from its place; but if for a time you leave it untouched, you will need a windlass to upheave it from its roots. You may stop the spring at its source with a bodkin; but the full stream you cannot ford on the back of an elephant.— *Ch. I.* 4.

O thou who art sated, to thee a barley-loaf will not seem sweet.

That which to me appeareth lovely, is in thy sight a deformity.

To the inhabitants of paradise, purgatory would be hell ;

Ask the inhabitants of hell, they would tell you it is paradise.—*Ch. I.* 7.

With the strong arm and the power of the wrist,
It is a crime to crush the palm of the helpless wretch.
Let him live in fear who shows no mercy to the fallen,
For if his foot should slip, no one will stretch out a hand to him.—*Ch. I.* 10.

Whoever hath sown the seed of evil, and expecteth from it good fruit, hath but an empty brain, and nourisheth but a vain conceit.—*Ch. I.* 10.

Take the cotton out of thine ear, and distribute justice to the people; for if thou dealest not justly, surely there will be a day of judgment.—*Ch. I.* 10.

The sons of Adam are limbs of one another, for in their creation they are formed of one substance.
When fortune bringeth affliction to a single member, not one of the rest remaineth without disturbance.
Thou who art without sorrow for the misery of another,
Thou deservest not to be named a son of Adam.—*Ch. I.* 10.

They have related that Nushirvan, the just, was
once at his hunting-seat, and was about to have some
game cooked. There was no salt, and a servant was
sent to the village to bring some. Nushirvan said,
" Let it be paid for, that it become not a custom, and
the village be ruined." They said, " From this small
quantity, what injury could spring?" He replied,
" The origin of injustice in the world was in small
things; but every one who came into it added thereto,
till it arrived at its present extremity." If from the
garden of the peasant the monarch take but a single
apple, his servants would tear up the whole tree from
its roots; and if the Sultan take but five eggs
unjustly, his soldiers will spit a thousand fowls. The
iniquitous tyrant remaineth only for a season; the
curse upon him remaineth for ever.—*Ch. I.* 19.

Call to mind what said the elephant-driver on the
banks of the Nile: " Wouldst thou know the condition of the ant under thy foot, think what would be
thine own under the foot of the elephant."—*Ch. I.* 22.

If injury cometh to thee from a fellow-creature, do
not grieve,

For from thy fellow-creatures proceedeth neither quiet nor trouble.

Know that from God is the difference of enemy and friend, for the hearts of both are alike in His keeping.

Though the arrow flieth from the bow, the wise man looketh to him who directeth it.—*Ch. I.* 24.

Beware of the sighs from a deeply-wounded soul, for the deep wound will at last break forth. So long as thou art able, crush not a single heart, for a sigh has power to overturn a world.—*Ch. I.* 26.

The king ought to be the guardian of the poor: though affluence be his, and the splendour of fortune. The sheep were not made for the sake of the shepherd; but the shepherd was intended for the service of the sheep.—*Ch. I.* 28.

A vizier said to Zu-'l-nur of Egypt: "Night and day I am occupied in the service of the Sultan, hoping for some good thing, and dreading punishment." Zu-'l-nur wept, and said: "If I had feared the great God as you have feared the King, I should have been counted in the number of the just."—*Ch. I.* 29.

Life's season flieth away like the wind over the desert.

Bitter and sweet, ugliness and beauty, alike pass away.

The tyrant imagined that he was committing violence on us;

The violence hath passed away from us, and will remain on his own neck.—*Ch. I.* 30.

To win the hearts of friends, scruple not to sell thy father's garden. To boil the pot of thy well-wisher hesitate not to burn thy very furniture.—*Ch. I.* 33.

In so much as thou art able, distress not the mind of anyone; the pathway of life is strewn with many a thorn. Assist thou the wretched poor man in his troubles, for thou also wilt have troubles of thine own.—*Ch. I.* 35.

Never will the wise call him a great man who speaketh ill of the truly great.

All these things, when once they have passed away, are nothing;

Fortune, and thrones, and decrees, and interdicts, and seizing, and holding.

Defame not those who are departed with a good name, that thine own good name may remain immortal. —*Ch. I.* 41.

FROM THE SECOND CHAPTER, ON THE QUALITIES OF DEVOTEES.

Whomsoever thou beholdest in the garment of piety, him believe to be pious; and treat as a good man, though thou knowest not what may be the inward disposition: what business has the policeman in the inside of the house?—*Ch. II.* 1.

I have heard that men who walk in the ways of God would not grieve the hearts even of their enemies. How can such eminence be reached by thee—thee, who art ever in strife and opposition with thy friends?—*Ch. II.* 4.

The love of the sincere is the same to your face and to your back, not such as of those

Who at your back find out your faults, but to your
face would die for you;
   Who in your presence are mild as the lamb,
   But in your absence are man-devouring wolves.—
Ch. II. 4.

Whoever brings to your notice and counts up the
defects of others, he, be sure, will display to others
those which he sees in you.—*Ch. II.* 4.

Who knows what manner of man the cloak dis-
guises!—the writer only knows the contents of the
letter.—*Ch. II.* 5.

O Arab! I fear thou wilt never reach the Holy
Place,
   For the road which thou art travelling leadeth
towards Tatary.—*Ch. II.* 6.

Thou who displayest thy virtues in the palm of
thine hand, but hidest thy vices under thine armpits,
what, O vain man, dost thou expect to purchase in
the day of anguish with thy counterfeit silver?—
Ch. II. 6.

I remember that in the season of childhood I was religiously minded, and inclined to the practice of abstemiousness and austerities. One night I was sitting in attendance on my father, and never closed my eyes the whole night. I held the precious volume to my bosom, but the company around us were all asleep. I said to my father : "Of all these not one lifts up the head to repeat the prayer." He replied : "Soul of thy father! better were it for thee that thou also wert asleep, than thus to be remarking on the faults of others."—*Ch. II.* 7.

The vain pretender sees nothing but himself, for the veil of self-conceit is before his eyes. Would anyone bestow upon his eye the power of discerning God, no one would he behold so weak as himself.— *Ch. II.* 7.

In the eyes of men of the world I am of a goodly aspect, but from my inward impurity I bow down my head in shame. Men will praise the peacock for his elegance and beauty, but he is himself ashamed of his ugly feet.— *Ch. II.* 8.

They asked Lokman from whom he learnt good manners. He replied: "From the ill-mannered. Whatever in their behaviour appeared to me disagreeable, that I refrained from doing myself."

Not a word can be said, even in child's play,

From which an intelligent person may not gather instruction ;

But if a hundred chapters of " Wisdom " were read in the hearing of a fool,

To his ears it would sound as nothing but child's play.—*Ch. II.* 21.

To one who was complaining to his spiritual guide how difficult it was to bear the slanders of injurious tongues, he replied in tears :—"How canst thou be sufficiently grateful for this blessing : that thou art better than they think thee ! How many times wilt thou keep repeating, 'The envious and malevolent are perpetually calumniating me, wretch that I am?' If they rise up to shed thy blood, or if they sit down to speak evil of thee, cease not thou to be good, and let them say on their evil. Better this than that thou shouldst be evil, and that they should repute thee good. Look at me, whom men regard as a model of perfection, whilst I know myself that I am imperfec-

tion itself. Had I really done what they report of
me, I had indeed been a virtuous and pious man!
The door closed in thine own face to exclude men
from thy presence, that they may not behold and
spread abroad thy faults—the closed door—of what
use is it before the Omniscient?—before Him, who
knows alike what is open and what is concealed?—

Yesternight, towards morning, a warbling bird stole
away my reason, my patience, my strength, and my
understanding. My exclamations, by chance, reached
the ear of a most intimate friend. "Never," he said,
could I have believed that the voice of a bird should
have such power to disturb thine intellect!" "It is
not," I replied, " befitting the condition of man, that
a bird should be reciting its hymn of praise, and that
I should be silent."—*Ch. II.* 26.

To celebrate Him all that thou beholdest is roused
to exclamation.

The heart to understand it becometh an ear.

Not only is the nightingale on the rose-bush
warbling its hymn of praise,

But every thorn becometh a tongue to laud his perfection.—*Ch. II.* 26 and 27.

Abu Hurairah (the satisfaction of God be with him,) used to come every day to offer his service to Mustafa, (*Mohammed,*) upon whom be the mercy and peace of God. One day the Prophet (on whom be a blessing,) said to him:—" Oh, Abu Hurairah, do not come *every* day, that our friendship may increase."

A holy man has said:—" With all the beauty which attends the sun, I have never heard, that any one has taken him for a friend, except in winter, when he is veiled, and *therefore* is loved."—*Ch. II.* 30.

There is no harm in paying visits to others, but go not so often that they say, " It is enough!"

If a man would learn to reprove himself, he would never hear reproof from any one else.—*h. II.* 30.

Whoever is possessed of the finer mind,—be he orator, or lawyer, or teacher, or scholar,—if once he descends to low, worldly greed, will find himself entangled like a fly in honey.—*h. II.* 33.

A pupil said to his instructor: " What am 1 to do? for people incommode me with the frequency of their visits to such a degree that their conversation pro-

duces a great distraction of my valuable time." He
replied: "To every one who is poor, lend; and from
every one who is rich, borrow: they will not come
about you again." —*Ch. II. 37.*

Turn not away, O holy man, thy face from the
sinner. Rather look upon him with benevolence. If
I have not been in my deeds all that a man ought to
be, come to my aid in the spirit of the generous.—
Ch. II. 40.

I saw some handfuls of fresh roses tied up with
grass on the top of a cupola. I said:
"What doth this worthless grass, to be sitting thus
in the rank of roses?"
The grass wept and replied: "Be silent!
The generous never forget their companionship.
Though I have no beauty, or colour, or odour, am
I not the grass of His garden?
I am the servant of the munificent Majesty,
nourished from of old by His fostering bounty.
Whether I have any virtue, or whether I have it
not.
Still am I hopeful of the mercy of my Master.

Although no valuable stock be mine; no wealth of worship—
He knoweth the remedy for his servant's case, when all other support faileth."—*Ch. II.* 48.

On the monument of Bahram Gur (*a Persian King*) was written:
"The liberal hand is better than the strong arm.
Hatim-Tai (*an Arabian chief, proverbial for his generosity*) liveth no more;
But to eternity his great name will remain renowned
On account of his liberality."
Distribute in alms the tithe of thy wealth; for the more the husbandman lops off the exuberance of the vine, the more it will yield of grapes.—*Ch. II.* 49.

FROM THE THIRD CHAPTER, ON THE EXCELLENCY OF CONTENTMENT.

An African mendicant, in the Mercers' Row at Aleppo, kept saying: "O wealthy sirs, if you had justice, and we contentment, the practice of begging would go out of the world."

O contentment, do thou make me rich!

For without thee there is no such thing as riches.— *Ch. III. 1.*

The treasure chosen by Lokman was patience; without patience, there is no such thing as wisdom.— *Ch. III. 1.*

One of the Kings of Persia sent an able physician into the service of Mohammed. He remained some years in Arabia, but no one came to consult him, or to ask for his medicines. One day he presented himself to the Prophet, complaining that he had been sent to heal his people, but that in all that time no one had paid him any attention. The prophet replied: " It is the custom of this nation not to eat till compelled by hunger, and to withdraw their hand from food whilst they have still an appetite." The physician said: " This is the reason that they are so healthy." So he made his obeisance, and departed.— *Ch. III.* 4.

In the Institutes of Ardshir Babegan, it is recorded that he asked an Arabian physician: "What quantity of food may one eat daily?" He answered: "A hundred direms in weight is sufficient." He said: " What strength could such a quantity give?" He replied: "This quantity will carry you, and whatever more you take you will have to carry."—*Ch. III.* 6.

They asked a sick man: " What does thy heart desire?" He replied: " That it might desire anything."—*Ch. III.* 9.

They asked Hatim Tai: "Hast thou ever seen in the world any one more noble-minded than thyself?" He replied: "One day I had offered a sacrifice of forty camels, and had gone out with some Arab chiefs to a corner of the desert. There I saw a thorn-cutter, who had gathered together a bundle of thorns. I said to him: 'Why goest thou not to share the hospitality of Hatim Tai, when a crowd has assembled at his feast? He replied: 'Whoever can eat the bread of his own labour will not put himself under an obligation to Hatim Tai.' This man in mind and in magnanimity I consider greater than myself."— *Ch. III.* 15.

Never had I complained of the vicissitudes of fortune, or saddened my face at the revolution of the heavens, except once on a time when my foot was naked, and I had not wherewithal to purchase a shoe. Entering the great Mosque of Nufah, I saw there a man who had no feet. Then I converted my lament into gratitude and praise for the goodness of God, and bore my want of shoes with patience.

A roasted fowl is less than pot-herbs in the eye of him who is already satiated;

To him who is needy and fainting, a boiled turnip is a roasted fowl.—*Ch. III.* 19.

———

I have heard of a wealthy man who was as notorious for his stinginess as was Hatim Tai for his liberality. No one ever saw his door open or his table spread. He was sailing on the Western sea on his way to Egypt, when a contrary wind assailed the ship. Then he lifted up his hand in prayer, and began to utter vain lamentations.

What advantage can the hand of supplication be to the unhappy servant,

Raised to God in the moment of peril, but when, liberality is needed, folded under the arm?—*Ch. III.* 23.

FROM THE FOURTH CHAPTER,
ON THE ADVANTAGES OF SILENCE.

I have heard one of the sages say : "No one con-
fesseth his own ignorance so much as the man who
beginneth to talk whilst another is speaking, and
hath not yet finished."—*Ch. IV. 7.*

I was hesitating about a contract for the purchase
of a house. A Jew said to me: "I am one of the
old householders of this quarter. I can tell you the
qualities of the house, and say to you, 'Buy ; it hath
no faults.'" I replied : "Except having you for a
neighbour."—*Ch. IV. 9.*

A man with a disagreeable voice, and in a loud tone, was reading the Koran. An observant passer-by asked, "What is your stipend?" "Nothing," he replied. "Why, then, give yourself this trouble?" "I read," he said, "for the sake of God." "Then," he replied, "for God's sake read no longer. You mar the beauty of your religion."—*Ch. IV.* 14.

FROM THE FIFTH CHAPTER,
ON LOVE AND YOUTH.

They asked Hussain Maimundi, how it was that Sultan Mahmud, who had so many handsome slaves, each one of whom was of rare beauty, should have no heart-felt affection for any of them, except for Iyâz, one who had no excess of comeliness. He replied,—"Hast thou not heard, that whatever toucheth the heart, will look fair to the eye?"

If any one regardeth another with the eye of dislike,

Tho' he were formed in the image of Joseph,

He would yet be looked upon as one of the unlovely;

And if thou regardest a demon with the eye of desire,

He would appear to thine eye an angel and a cherub.

Whomsoever the Sultan regardeth with partiality,

All that he doeth badly is sure to be well done ;
And whomsoever the Monarch discardeth from his presence,
Will never be caressed by any one of the house-hold.—*Ch. V.* 1.

———

There was a handsome and virtuous youth
Who was betrothed to a beautiful girl.
I have read that as they were sailing on the great sea,
They fell together into a whirlpool.
When a sailor came to seize his hand, and save him from perishing in that extremity,
He called out from the midst of the threatening waves, "Leave hold of me and take the hand of my beloved."
Every one admired him for that speech, and when he was expiring he was heard to say,
" Learn not the tale of love from that light-minded man who forgetteth his beloved in the hour of danger."—*Ch. V.* 21.

FROM THE SIXTH CHAPTER, ON WEAKNESS AND OLD AGE.

It was good, the answer which the aged woman made to her son, when she beheld him, strong as an elephant, able to cope with a tiger; "Didst thou call to remembrance the time of thine infancy, when thou layest helpless in my embrace, thou wouldst not to-day afflict me with violence, thou in the fulness of thy manhood, and I a weak old woman.—*Ch. VI.* 6.

A rich but avaricious man had a son who was sick. The well-wishers said: " It would be well to recite over him a chapter of the Holy Book, or to offer a sacrifice and distribute to the poor: perchance God might restore his health." For a moment he became thoughtful and then said: "It is better to read a chapter, which can be done in an instant; my flock is at a distance." An intelligent fellow who heard this, said: "He prefers the Holy Book, because it is on the tip of his tongue, whilst his gold is at the bottom of his heart."—*Ch. VI.* 7.

FROM THE SEVENTH CHAPTER,
ON THE EFFECTS OF EDUCATION.

He who hath never learned good habits in his childhood, will in his manhood never recover his superiority.
You may twist the green wood in any way you please;
the dry you can make straight only by fire.—*Ch.
VII.* 3.

A king who was sending his son to school, placed
on his breast a silver tablet, on which was written,
in letters of gold: "The severity of the school-
master is better than the indulgence of the father."—
Chap. VII. 4.

I heard a learned instructor saying to one of his scholars : " Did a man fix his heart as much upon Him who affords him subsistence as upon the subsistence itself, he would raise himself into the sphere of angels.

He did not forget thee when thou wert as yet unformed and hidden in the womb.

He gave thee a soul, and reason, and form, and intellect,

And beauty, and speech, and thought, and judgment, and understanding.

He arranged on thine hands thy ten fingers, and adapted thy two arms to thy shoulders,

And thinkest thou now, who art at thy best a mere nothing, that He will forget to give thee means of subsistence."—*Ch. VII. 7.*

I saw an Arab, who was saying to his son : " O, my child, on the day of the resurrection they will ask you, What have you done? not—Whose son are you ? The veil which they kiss in the Holy Place is not famous, because it came from the silkworm. It was associated some time with a venerable personage: that is the reason why it is so precious."—*Ch. VII. 8.*

A silly fellow having a pain in his eyes, went to a farrier, and asked him for a remedy. The farrier applied to his eyes something which he would have given to an animal, and it blinded him, upon which they made an appeal to the magistrate. The magistrate said: " This is no case for damages; it is plain that this fellow is an ass, or he would not have gone to a farrier." No man of enlightened understanding will commit weighty matters to one of mean abilities. A weaver of mats, though he be a weaver, will not be employed in the weaving of silk.—*Ch. VII.* 14.

One of the great had a worthy son. He died, and they asked him, "What shall we write on his tomb?" " He replied: " If it be necessary to write anything, this couplet will be sufficient—

" 'Woe is me! When the green herbs were blooming in the garden, how joyous was my heart!

" ' Pass by, O my friend, in the next spring, and thou wilt see the green herbs blowing out of my clay.' "—*Ch. VII.* 15.

A holy man, passing by one of the favourites of fortune, saw that he had bound one of his slaves tightly hand and foot, and was inflicting upon him severe punishment. He said, " O my son, the good and great God has subjected a creature like thyself to thy power, and has given to thee superiority over him. Be grateful for the benefits he has conferred on thee, and inflict not on him this violence, lest in the resurrection he be found better than thou art, and thou be brought to shame.

Be not over much angry with thy slave;

Treat him not unjustly, and pain not his feelings.

True, thou mayest have bought him for ten direms;

But 'twas not by thy power that he was created.

There is a tradition of the Prophet—peace be upon him!—that on the day of the resurrection the greatest grief will be when the pious slave is carried to Paradise, and his worthless master is borne away to Hell.—*Ch. VII.* 16.

———

I saw the son of a rich man seated at the head of his father's tomb, and engaged in a dispute with the son of a poor man. " The monument over my father's grave," said he, " is of marble; the inscription upon it in coloured letters; and the foundation is of stone, overlaid with azure tiles. What likeness is there between it and thy father's, which is two or three bricks packed together, with nothing but a handful or two of earth cast over it ?"—" Silence !" replied the poor man's son ; for whilst your father is striving to move under this heavy stone, my father will have arrived at Paradise.—*Ch. VII.* 18.

Of what utility are the rich, if they are clouds of August, and do not rain upon any one; or the fountain of the sun, and do not give light to any one ; or are mounted on the steed of power, and never make a charge ; advance not a foot in the service of God ; bestow not a direm without weighing it and distressing you ; watch over their wealth drudgingly, and leave it grudgingly ? And the sages have said that the silver of the miser comes up from the ground at the same moment that he himself goes down into the ground. One brings his money within his grasp anxiously and laboriously, and another comes and carries it away quietly and painlessly.—*Ch. VII.* 20.

Have a care that thou throw not away thy shield at the attack of the rhetorician, for his only weapons

are his borrowed exaggerations. Hold fast thy faith
and thy knowledge, for this skilful-in-words, and
this utterer of mellifluous cadences, shows arms at
the gate, but hath no defender within the castle.—
Ch. VII. 20.

FROM THE EIGHTH CHAPTER,
MAXIMS FOR THE CONDUCT OF LIFE.

Riches are for the comfort of life: not life for the amassing of riches. I asked a wise man who is the fortunate, and who is the unfortunate man? He replied: "He is the fortunate who sowed and reaped, and he the unfortunate who died and enjoyed not. Offer no prayer in behalf of that worthless wretch, who did nothing but spend his life in the accumulation of wealth which he used not!"—*Ch. VIII.* 1.

Wouldst thou be the better for worldly possessions, be beneficent to others, as God has been beneficent to thee. The Arabs say: "Give, and account it not an obligation, for the advantage of it will come back to thyself."

Wherever the tree of liberality has rooted itself, its stem and its branches will ascend to the sky.

If thou hast hopes of eating of its fruit, deem it not an obligation that thou didst not lay the axe to its root.

Be thankful to God that he has prospered thee to thy good,

And has not shut thee out from a share in his favours. Think not that thou conferrest an obligation in serving the Sultan ;

Recognise the obligation he has conferred upon thee by placing thee in his service.—*Ch. VIII. 2.*

———

Two persons took trouble in vain, and laboured without advantage—he who gained wealth which he enjoyed not, and he who gathered knowledge which he did not apply. Whatever amount of science you may possess, if you reduce it not to practice you are still ignorant. The boast which you load with a few books is not on that account a learned man or a philosopher. What knows that empty skull, whether it be carrying precious volumes or firewood ?—*Ch. VIII. 3.*

Three things are not stable without three things—
wealth without traffic; learning without discussion;
and a kingdom without government.—*Ch. VIII. 7.*

Thou shouldst speak such words between two
enemies that, should they become friends, thou wilt
not need be ashamed. A quarrel between two persons
is like a fire, and he who malevolently reports their
words is like one who supplies fuel to the flame.
Speak softly to your friends, that the blood-thirsty
enemy may not overhear. Be on your guard when
you speak before a wall, that there be not an ear
behind the wall.—*Ch. VIII.* 12.

Whilst an affair can be arranged with money, it is
not right to endanger life; nor till every device has
failed does it become law to lay hands upon the
sword.—*Ch. VIII. 15.*

The wicked man is a captive in the hand of an
enemy, for whithersoever he goeth he cannot free
himself from the grasp of his own punishment.

If the wicked man should seek refuge in heaven from his anguish,

He would still be in anguish from his own evil disposition.—*Ch. VIII. 21.*

———

Hearest thou news which will afflict a heart, be thou silent, and let another bear it. O nightingale! bring thou the good news of the spring; leave to the owl the tidings of evil.—*Ch. VIII. 25.*

———

He who offers advice to a self-conceited man needs himself advice from another.—*Ch. VIII. 25.*

———

An affair succeeds through patience, and over-haste ends in disappointments. I have seen with my own eyes in the desert the slow man pass by the quick one; the wind-footed courser fall exhausted through its speed, and the camel-driver, though tardily, push on to the end.—*Ch. VIII. 35.*

———

To the ignorant man nothing is better than silence, and were he aware of this, he would no longer be ignorant.

When you are not possessed of perfection or excellence,

It is better that you keep your tongue within your mouth.

The tongue bringeth disgrace upon men. The nut without a kernel is light in weight.

The beast will not learn of thee how to speak; learn thou of the beast how to be silent.

Whoever reflecteth not before he answereth,

Will probably utter inappropriate words.

Either adorn thy speech with the intelligence of a man,

Or sit in silence like a dumb animal.—*Ch. VIII.* 36.

Whoever entereth into argument, in order to display his learning, with a man more learned than himself, will thereby be taught that he is unlearned. Though thou mayest be well informed, if one wiser than thyself take up the discourse, be not thou ready to start objections.—*Ch. VIII.* 37.

Publish not the secret faults of others, for you inflict disgrace upon them, and procure thereby no honour to yourself.—*Ch. VIII.* 39.

He who readeth and doth not practice, resembleth the man who driveth the oxen, but scattereth not the seed.—*Ch. VIII.* 40.

Were every night a night of power, "THE NIGHT OF POWER" would lose its worth. Were every pebble a ruby, the ruby and the pebble would be of equal value.—*Ch. VIII.* 43. (*Note* 1.)

It is very easy to deprive the living of life;
To give back life to him from whom thou hast taken it is impossible.
The archer should be patient ere he draw the bow,
For when the arrow hath left the bow it returneth no more.—*Ch. VIII.* 54.

What wonder if the nightingale lose its spirit, if a crow is the companion of its cage.—*Ch. VIII.* 55.

The friend whom it hath taken a lifetime to acquire, it is not right to estrange in a moment. How many years doth it require to turn the stone into a ruby? Take heed lest with another stone thou grind it down in an instant.—*Ch. VIII.* 57.

I heard a fellow of mean disposition slandering a person of distinguished rank. I said: " O, sir! if thou art unfortunate, why is it a crime to be one of the fortunate? Oh! do not invoke misery on the envious man, for the condition of that man is misery in itself. What need of pursuing one with emnity, who has such an enemy perpetually at his heels?"— *Ch. VIII.* 70.

I asked a wise man to give me a word of counsel. He said to me: " Take heed how you commit yourself with an ignorant man, for if you are possessed of knowledge you will become an ass, and if you are without knowledge, your folly will become still greater."—*Ch. VIII.* 80.

The bird will not alight upon the seed,
If it see another bird caught in the snare.
Take thou warning from the misfortunes of others,
That thou give no occasion to others to take
warning from thee.—*Ch. VIII.* 90.

The poor man whose end is good is better than the king whose end is evil.

The sorrow which thou bearest before enjoyment
Is better than the enjoyment which precedeth sorrow.
—*Ch. VIII.* 92.

A holy man in his prayers was wont to say: " O
God, have mercy on the bad, for on the good Thou
hast already had mercy, in that Thou hast created
them good."—*Ch. VIII.* 98.

Feridoon ordered his Chinese embroiderers to
embroider around his 'pavilion : " Thou who art of
an understanding heart be good to the wicked,
for the good are great and happy of themselves."—
Ch. VIII. 99.

Two persons died, carrying with them vain regrets ;
he who had wealth which he never enjoyed, and he
who had knowledge of which he made no use.—
Ch. VIII. 106.

No one ever saw a man who had merit, but was
miserly, that people did not expatiate on his faults ;
but if a generous man hath two hundred defects, his
generosity will cover them all.—*Ch. VIII.* 106.

Generosity and kindness make the man; think not that it is his material image. To gain all the wealth of the world is not virtue; try if thou canst conquer a single heart.

The truly wise man practiceth humility; the bough full of fruit inclineth its head towards the ground. It is in those of high estate that humility appeareth to most advantage; in the beggar it is only the mark of his profession.—*From the Pend-Nameh, or Book of Counsels.*

PART II.

FLOWERS FROM THE

BOSTAN, OR PLEASURE GARDEN.

IF THOU SOWEST THORNS THOU WILT NOT REAP JESSAMINE.

CROWDS ARE THERE OF THOSE, WHO GREEDY OF THE WORLD'S PLEASURES THINK THAT NOT HAVING SCATTERED THE GRAIN THEY CAN YET GATHER THE HARVEST.

BUT SADI TELLS YOU, ONLY HE WHO SCATTERETH THE SEED WILL REAP THE HARVEST.—*The Bostán.*

FROM THE BOSTAN, OR PLEASURE-GROUND, OF SADI.

Invocation.

In the name of God—the Merciful, the Compassionate.

In the name of the Lord, who created the soul;
who gave to the tongue words of wisdom;
The Lord, the Benevolent, the Sustainer, who
generously accepteth excuses, and forgiveth sins;
The Mighty One, from whose door whoever turneth
away, will find Might at no other door;
In whose court the most exalted Monarchs must
humble themselves as suppliants;
Who is not quick to repress the arrogant, nor
repulseth with violence those who sue for pardon;

Who, when He is angry for some evil deed, if thou turnest to Him again, writeth it amongst the things of the past;

Who, when He beholdeth the sin, covereth it with the veil of His mercy ; in the ocean of whose omniscience the universe is but a drop.

If a son is at variance with a father, thou wilt immediately behold the father in the glow of passion;

And if he doth not soon give him satisfaction, will drive him forth from his presence like a stranger.

If the slave doth not bestir himself actively at his work, his master will deem him but of little value.

Or, if thou art not amiable amongst thy companions, thy companions will flee from thee to a mile's distance.

Or, if a soldier deserteth his duty, his commander will speedily dismiss him from the service.

But He who is Lord of the high and of the low, shutteth not the door of His riches against even the rebellious.

The expanse of the earth is the table of His people; and to His free banquet friend and foe are alike welcome.

If He hurried to involve him in trouble, who would be secure from the hand of His power?

Independent in His essence of the judgment of any one of His creatures, His dominion is rich in the obedience of men and spirits.

Every thing, and every person must bow down to his mandate : the sons of Adam, and the bird, and the ant, and the worm.

So broadly is the table of His bounty spread, that the vulture on the Caucasus receiveth his portion.

Benevolent, and beneficent, and the dispenser of blessings, He is the Lord of Creation, and knoweth every secret.

This man He judgeth worthy of grandeur and a high destiny, for his kingdom is ancient, and his race is wealthy.

On the head of one He setteth the diadem of fortune; another He bringeth down from a throne to the dust.

On the head of one He placeth the crown of prosperity : another He clotheth in the weeds of poverty.

For His friend (Abraham) He turned fire into a bed of roses ; and cast into the flames the host from the waters of the Nile. (*Note* 2.)

If He did that, it was marked with His favour; and if He did this, it was signed with His order.

He throweth His veil over evil deeds, and hideth behind it His own benefits :

If He unsheatheth His sword of power in wrath, the very Cherubim are dumb with terror :

But if He giveth victuals from the table of His bounty, even the Evil-One says—"I too shall have a portion."

In the court of His benignity and greatness, the greatest must lay their greatness aside ;

But to such as are cast down, He is nigh with His mercy, and He ever lendeth His ear to the prayer of the suppliant.

By His prescience He foreseeth what hath not yet been ; in His goodness He provideth for what hath not yet been spoken.

By His power He is the keeper of the heights and the depths, and He is master of the Book of the Day of Account.

No one's back is strong enough to throw off obedience ; nor is there room for any one to lay a finger on a letter.

The Ancient Benefactor is still ever beneficent ; by decree upon decree He fashioned the beautiful image in the womb.

From east to west he set in motion sun and moon, and spread out the earth on the face of the waters.

And though it trembleth sometimes and dreadeth

its ruin, He hath nailed down the roots of the mountains to its skirts.

He who hath imprinted its form upon the waters, gave to the pearl its Peri-like semblance.

He hid the ruby and the turquoise in the bosom of the stone, and hung the ruby-coloured rose on the turquoise-tinted branches.

He directeth the drops from the cloud to the ocean, and the seed of the father to the womb of the mother.

Of one globule He maketh a pearl-white lily, and fashioneth another into the lofty cypress.

From His knowledge not an atom lieth concealed, for the hidden and open are both to Him but one.

For the ant and for the serpent he hath alike provided its food, and for that which hath no hand, nor feet, nor strength.

At His decree non-existence hath been embellished with existence, for no one knoweth but He how to change nonentity into being.

So at one time He burieth an act in silence, and bringeth it forth again in the plain of the last judgment.

The universe is agreed in the acknowledgment of His Deity, but is confounded when it attempteth to investigate His Essence.

Man cannot comprehend the extent of His Majesty, the sight hath not penetrated to the limits of His excellence.

The wing of bird hath not soared to the summits of His knowledge, nor the hand of intelligence touched the skirts of His attributes.

In this whirlpool have been sunk a thousand vessels, of which not a single plank hath come to the shore.

How many a night have I sat completely lost, till I have exclaimed in terror—" Up, and be doing."

Of the kingdoms of the earth the knowledge is attainable, but the knowledge of Him, with thy measure, thou canst not attain.

The bounds of His knowledge thine intellect cannot reach ; nor can thy thoughts fathom the depths of His attributes.

To equal Sohlan in eloquence is possible, but innumerable are they who have fallen exhausted in the race.

To urge thy steed over every ground is impossible, and there are occasions on which thou must throw away thy shield.

If the traveller is forbidden to penetrate to the secret place, he will find the door barred, and will have to return.

To many a one at this banquet is offered the goblet, who findeth it to be but a stupifying drug.

Let every one tremble who hath trusted himself to this ocean of blood, from which no one yet ever brought back his vessel.

One falcon soareth up, but with bandaged eyes; another returneth, but with singed eyes and feathers.

No one hath found his way to the treasure of Karun; or, if he hath found it, hath he brought anything back.

Seekest thou to survey this country, as well mayest thou begin by hamstringing the horse on which thou wouldest return.

Let each one look into the mirror of his own soul, and gradually it will acquire the same clearness.

Perhaps the odour of love will inebriate thee, and, seeking for a compact with the divine, thou mayest thyself become divine.

Proceed on the road of inquiry on foot, till thou reach the goal; and thence fly upwards on the pinions of affection.

Truth will rend in twain the veils of illusion; yea, even the veil which concealeth the glory of God.

But the courser of intellect can run no further! Astonishment tighteneth the reins, and exclaimeth— " STAND !"—*Graf's Text, Vienna,* 1858, *p.* 2. *Transl. Jena,* 1850, I. 1.

FROM BOOK THE FIRST,
ON UPRIGHTNESS AND GOVERNMENT.

The Tiger-tamer.

They relate a story of one of the great in faith—one searching after the truth, and with an eye for the real—

That he beheld a pious man, riding along rapidly and grasping a serpent in his hand.

One who was passing by exclaimed—"O thou who art journeying on the way towards God, direct me too on the road on which thou art travelling!

"What hast thou done to tame the ravenous beast, and stamp on thy name the seal of felicity?"

He replied—"If I have subdued the tiger, the serpent, the elephant, or the vulture, be not thou astonished!

"Thou too withdraw not thy neck from the All-Ruler, and no one will withdraw his neck from thy rule."

When the Monarch submitteth himself to the commands of the Law-Giver, God will become to him a guardian and defender;

And when the All-Righteous is become thy friend, it is impossible that He should deliver thee into the hand of thine enemy.

This is the right way; turn not thy face from it; make this thy desire, and what thou desirest, thou wilt find.—*Graf's Text, p.* 29. *Transl. I.* 19.

The Last Words of Nushirvan.

I have heard that at the moment when the soul was departing, thus spake Nushirvan to his son Hormuz:

" Be thou in heart the guardian of the poor; be not in bondage to thine own ease.

" No one will live in comfort in thy kingdom, if thou desirest only thine own comfort, and sayest— ' That is enough !'

" He will receive no praise from the wise, who passeth his nights in sleep whilst the wolf is amidst the flock.

" Keep watch over the necessitous poor, for the peasant it is from whom the king deriveth his throne.

" The king is the tree, the peasant is the root: the tree, O my son, deriveth its strength from the root."— *Graf's Text, p.* 31.   *Transl. I.* 19.

Kingly Actions.

Hast thou displaced any one from his office, after a season forgive him his fault.

To fulfil the expectations of one to whom thou hast given hopes, is better than to break the chains of a thousand slaves.

The just king will bear himself towards those who are under his orders, as a father who hath cause for anger with his son.

Sometimes he will strike him so as to inflict pain; sometimes he will drop the crystal water from his eyes.

If thou art too soft, thine adversary will wax too bold; if thou art too harsh, he will fly from thee.

Better are softness and harshness together, as the surgeon applieth at once the knife and the plaster.

Be thou generous, and gentle, and forgiving; as God hath scattered upon thee, so scatter thou upon others.

No one hath come into the world for continuance, save him who leaveth behind him a good name.

Nor hath any one died who hath left as an inheritance a bridge, a mosque, an hostel, or an hospital.

Whoever hath left no such memorial behind him, his existence hath been but that of a tree which never bore fruit.

And whoever hath departed and left no mark, his name after his death will never be lauded.—*Graf's Text, p.* 39.   *Transl. I.* 25.

Kingly Duties.

It is no crime to drink water without the command of the law; but if thou sheddest blood, it must not be done without a decree.

If the law pronounce its decree, then thou mayest slay the criminal without any dread :

But if thou hast those who belong to his family, them forgive, and extend to them thy mercy.

The iniquitous man it was who committed the crime; what was the offence of his helpless wife and children ?

Is thy person powerful and thine army great, make not on that account an inroad upon the lands of thine enemy ;

He will flee away to his lofty castle, and thou wilt ruin only his unoffending country.

Look well into the circumstances of thy prisoners, for possibly there may be amongst them those who are innocent.

If a merchant die in thy dominions, it is unjust to lay thine hand upon his property.

For afterwards, when they raise over him the cry
of lamentation, they will unite in exclamations :—
" The unhappy man died a stranger in thy country,
and a tyrant robbed him of what remained of his
goods."

Think of that little fatherless child, and dread the
sigh of his miserable heart.

Oft times the fair name of fifty years a single ugly
deed hath ruined for ever.

Though a man be king from one end of the earth
to the other, when he taketh away the wealth of the
prosperous he is but a beggar.

Rather will the generous man die with an empty
hand, than fill his stomach from the pittance of the
poor.—*Graf's Text, p.* 57.   *Transl. I.* 38.

The Frugal Monarch.

I have heard of a just and commanding Ruler, whose cloak was of coarse serge within and without.

Some one exclaimed to him—"O thou who wast born on a fortunate day, order thyself a robe of brocade of China."

He replied—"This stuff is sent for comfort and raiment. What goeth beyond this is all for display and ornament.

"It is not for that purpose that I take the taxes— to embellish myself, my throne, and my diadem.

"Were I to clothe my body with robes like women, how should I have the manliness to repel my enemies?

"I have myself a hundred kinds of avarice and passions, but my treasury is not for myself alone.

"My treasury must be full for the sake of mine army, not for the object of beauty and ornament."

The soldier who is not made light-hearted by the King, will hardly guard well the boundaries of the kingdom.

When the enemy hath carried off the ass of the villager, why should the King be eating the tithes and the taxes?

The enemy hath borne away the ass, and the Sultan the tillage; what good is there in store for such a crown and throne!

Violence towards one who hath fallen is not manly; 'tis to be the base bird that snatcheth the grain from the emmet!

The peasant is a tree which, if thou wilt nurture it, will yield thee fruit to the hearts'-desire of thy friends.

Do not ruthlessly uproot it and destroy its produce; for so doing, the foolish man doeth an injury to himself.

Whoso dealeth not harshly with his subject will eat of his fruit in cheerfulness and prosperity;

But if the subject be pushed down from his footing, be afraid of his lamenting appeal to God.

If it be allowed thee to take a city by gentle means, pour not out blood from the veins in battle;

To subjugate by thy valour every kingdom of the earth, it would not be worth while that a drop of blood should trickle to the ground.—*Graf's Text, p.* 59. *Transl.* I. 40.

Inscription on the Fountain of Jemshid.

I have heard that Jemshid, of happy disposition, inscribed on a tablet at the head of a fountain:

Many like ourselves have breathed at this fountain, and departed, and closed their eyes upon it.

They captured the world by courage, or violence, but carried away with them nothing to the grave.

They departed each one, and of that which they had tilled nothing remained to them save a good or an evil name.

When thine enemy hath fallen into thine hands, grieve him not further, he hath already tasted enough of sorrow.

Better hold in thy keeping a discomfited enemy alive, than to have on thy neck the stain of his blood.
—*Graf's Text. p.* 61. *Transl. I.* 41.

The Grandee and the Beggar.

An exalted personage who dwelt in Irâk, heard a poor wretch exclaim beneath his balcony :

"There is a door at which thou art hopeful of entering; give hope then to those who sit asking at thine."

Dost thou desire that thine own heart should not suffer, redeem thou the sufferer from the bonds of misery.

The heart-piercing anguish of the petitioner for justice hath been enough to eject a monarch from his kingdom.

Thou sleepest at mid-day in the coolness of thine harem, and sayest to the poor stranger—" Go, thou, and be scorched in the burning noon."

But God will do justice in behalf of the man who implored in vain the justice of the king.—*Graf's Text,* p. 64. *Graf's Transl. I.* 43.

Tokiah's Councillor.

In the chronicles of the elder kings it is written, that when Tokiah sat upon the throne of Zengi;

In his time no one suffered injury from another: each took precedence as he was equally good, and that was enough.

To an affectionate companion he one day said: " Life is coming to an end, and without aught of profit.

Since royalty, and dignities, and thrones pass away, and no one carrieth anything out of the world except the Devotee,

I will seat myself in the cell of adoration, that I may discover the meaning of this brief existence."

When his enlightened friend heard him say this, he exclaimed excitedly and with some asperity, " Madman! hold! enough!

There is no devotion save in the service of others; it consisteth not in the prayer-carpet, in rosaries, or in the garb of the Derwish.

Be on the throne of sovereignty THYSELF, and in the purity of thy morals be the Derwish.

Gird thy loins with truthfulness and good purposes; and keep thy tongue tied from doubtful words and questionings.

Thy way is by the foot, not by the mouth; for words without action have no substance.

The eminent ones who distributed the ready-money of pure deeds had the Derwish's tatters under their proper garments."—*Graf's Text, p.* 68.*Transl. I.* 46.

Reply of a Devotee to a complaining Sultan.

I have heard that one of the Sultans of Rûm thus poured out his tearful lamentation :

" Nothing now remaineth within my power : nothing is left me save this city and castle.

Many an effort did I make, that my children after me might become a numerous and powerful lineage ;

Now a malignant enemy hath obtained the mastery, and turned from me all aid and the fruit of my labour.

What plan shall I adopt ? what remedy apply ? for the soul within my body is dwindling away with anguish !"

He replied—" O brother, swallow thy grief; for the larger and better portion of thy life is gone already !

Enough is still left for what remaineth ; when thou art departed, the world will be the place of another.

Be he wise or be he ignorant, devour not his grief, —he will assuredly have his own to devour.

To possess the world, it is not worth the trouble to take it with the sword and then to leave it.

Whom knowest thou of the Khosrus of Persia, of the age of Feridun, of Zohak, or Jemshid, whose throne and whose kingdom hath not come to ruin!

Naught save His sovereignty—the great God's—remaineth for ever!

Who can have the hope of enduring eternally, when thou beholdest not one who endureth for ever!

If thou keepest thy gold and silver, thy goods and thy treasure, after a few days they will be trodden under foot :

But he whose soul abideth in goodness, from moment to moment will find mercy to his soul.

The great man who leaveth behind him a good name will indubitably live in the memory of the generous.

Of a surety, if thou nurturest the tree of nobility, thou mayest certainly hope to eat of its fruit.

Let then thine aspirations be ever towards the noble; for when the Demons assign the habitations,

They will assign them only to the meed of excellence.

To the one who hath been the most forward in good deeds, the loftiest station in the Courts of God ;

Whilst he who hath been faithless will veil himself in shame at asking for the reward of actions unperformed.

Shame on the man—his teeth should gnaw his hand—who had the hot oven, and did not bake his loaf!

When thou knowest the time for gathering in the grain, not to have sown the seed was wilful transgression!—*Graf's Text, p.* 69.   *Transl. I.* 47.

Unselfishness.

If the merchant is awakened by the sound of the trumpet, what knoweth he of how the watchers have passed the night?

And if the traveller hath to bear the affliction of his own burthen, his heart is not troubled about the poor back-galled ass.

But, I perceive, that thou art not one of the fallen: wherefore, then, when thou see'st another fall, art thou standing still?

Once upon a time there was so sterile a year in Damascus, that friends forgot their natural affections.

The sky was so niggardly to the earth, that neither palm tree nor cornfield moistened its lip with water.

The source of the ancient fountains was dried up, and no water remained save the water in the eye of the orphan.

Nothing was heard save the sigh of the widowed woman, nor did smoke rise out of any chimney.

I saw the tree without leaves, naked as the body of the Derwish; the strength of the arm gone and turned into utter weakness.

On the mountain was no green, and the garden was a desert; the locust devoured the grove, and man the locust.

In this state of things I met a friend on whose bones nothing remained but the skin.

Once he had been strong and powerful; the possessor of rank and property and gold.

I said to him, " O my excellent friend, what misery hath come upon thee? Tell me!"

He thundered out,—"Whither are gone thy wits? To know, and to ask how! Thy question is a sin!"

" See'st thou not that the scarcity hath risen to its height?—That the calamity hath arrived at the bounds of extremity?"

No rain cometh down from the sky : nor doth the sigh of the groaner travel in the path of his desire."

I said to him,—" But thou, thou at least, hast no cause for dread : the poison killeth in the spot where is no antidote."

Should others die from want of means, for thee there is a rock; what fear of the deluge!"

My teacher looked at me grieved, with the look that one casteth upon silly people.

Comrade, if a man be safe upon the beach, will he be at rest whilst his friends are drowning?

Not from my own want of means is my face wan; wan is my face for the necessities of others.

The thoughtful man wisheth not to see a wound, either on his own limb, or on that of another.

Even when I am of sound body myself, when I see the wound of another, my body is all in a tremble.

The pleasure of that soundness is turned to misery, if one is beside me enfeebled by sickness.

When I see the poor wretch who hath nothing to eat, the morsel on my palate becometh gall and poison.

If I behold one of my friends borne away to prison, what would be left of the pleasure of walking in my pleasure-grounds?"—*Grif's Text*, *p.* 76. *Transl. I.* 52.

Selfishness.

One night the sighs of the people kindled a fire, and Bagdad, I have heard, was half burnt down.

"God be praised!"—cried one in the midst of it quickly—"that my shop hath suffered no injury."

One who had seen the world replied,—"O selfish man, who thinkest that it is enough to bear thine own grievance,

And art satisfied that a lofty city should be burnt to the ground, so only thine own house be saved!"

Who except a stony-hearted man could endure to fill his own stomach, whilst a stone lieth heavy on the stomach of another?

How can the rich man eat that morsel, when he seeth the poor man eating blood?

Say not that the watcher by the sick man is in health, for the watcher himself twitcheth at every pang of the sick man.

The travellers who arrive weary at the resting place can they sleep whilst the utterly worn-out are lagging behind?

Even the heart of a monarch must be burthened,

when he see'th the poor thorn-laden ass sticking in the clay.

To him who is seated in the palace of felicity even a syllable of one of Sadi's sayings is enough:

Equally so to thee then, if thou wilt listen to it, should be this:—"If thou sowest thorns, thou wilt not reap jessamine."—*Graf's Text, p.* 78. *Transl. I.* 54.

The Poor Man's Burthen is less heavy than the King's.

Say not that there is nothing higher than the Sultan's dignity; that the mendicant is not happier than the king!

The lightly-laden will move the lighter; and this is the truth, and pious men will listen to it.

The empty handed may eat his bread in sorrow; the king hath to devour the griefs of a world.

The beggar when he hath eaten his evening's crust sleepeth as sweetly as doth the Sultan of Syria.

Joy and sorrow alike come to an end; in death they depart both of them together,

What mattereth it that on the head of the one was placed a crown; that on the neck of the other were laid the taxes;

That the head of the one was exalted to Saturn; that the other lay poverty-stricken in a dungeon!

When the troop of Destiny fell upon them both, it was not possible to distinguish the one from the other.

Calamity is guardian of the Kingdom of Fortune; the beggar is a king, and the king a beggar.

I have heard that once upon a time a skull thus spake in the grave-yard to a holy man :—

"Once I possessed all the splendour ef sovereignty: the crown of greatness beamed upon my head.

I had armies to back me, and the favour of Fortune, and I conquered Irâk by the strong arm of Destiny ;

I had an eager desire to devour Kirmân also, but my head was itself devoured by worms!

Take the cotton of heedlessness out of the ear of thine intellect, that thine ear may receive counsel from the dead!"—*Graf's Text, p.* 86. *Transl. I.* 60.

BOOK THE SECOND,
ON BENEVOLENCE AND COMPASSION.

If thou art intelligent, prove thou the real for the real is the permanent : not so the image !

Whoso hath not knowledge and benevolence, and piety, knoweth nothing of reality, dwelleth only in the semblance.

He will sleep peacefully beneath the sod, who hath caused others to sleep with peaceful hearts.

Whilst thou still livest, consume thine own grief, for thine heir will not leave anything when dead.

Bestow thou then thy gold and thy wealth whilst they are thine, for when thou art gone they will be no longer in thy power.

And dost thou desire not to be hopeless for thyself, dismiss not from thy thoughts those who are forlorn.

Distribute thy treasure readily to-day, for to-morrow the key may no longer be in thine hand.

Make thou thyself provision for thy journey, for compassion of wife or child will not avail thee.

He who hath carried with him his heritage in eternity, he it is who hath borne from the world the ball of fortune.

Exert thyself to cast a covering over the poor, that God's own veil may be a covering for thee.

Turn not the stranger from thy door without his portion, lest thou thyself stand a stranger at the door of others.

Look thou with pity on the condition of the heart, for one day it may be thine own lot to be heart-broken.

Try to make joyful the soul of the desponding, and remember the day of despondency for thyself.

Thou hast not to stand a petitioner at the gate of others; in gratitude drive not the petitioner from thy gate. —*Graf's Text, p.* 138.   *Transl. I.* 96.

Orphanage.

Cast thy shade over the head of the fatherless: wipe away the dust from him ; draw out his thorn.

Knowest thou not what hath so sadly distressed him ?—Can the tree ever be fresh and green without its root ?

When thou beholdest the orphan cast down before thee, kiss not the face of thine own child.

If the orphan weepeth, who is there to caress him ? And if he is angry, who is there to soothe him ?

Take care that he weepeth not, for when the orphan weepeth even the throne of the Supreme trembleth.

Tenderly wipe away the tear from his eye, gently remove the dust from his face.

If his own shade no longer screeneth his head, do thou receive and nurture him under thine.

Once my head was encircled with a diadem, when my head reposed on the breast of a father.

If but a fly settled on my body, of how many about me were the hearts disquieted !

Now, were an enemy to cast me into prison, not one of my friends would come nigh to assist me.

I have experienced myself the sorrows of children,
for in childhood I lost the protection of my father.

The Lord of Khojund, who had once extracted a
thorn from an orphan's foot, appeared to some one in
a dream,

And said, as he paced the meads above,—" How
many roses have bloomed for me from that thorn !"
Graf's Text, p. 140.   *Trans. I.* 97.

Abraham and the Fire-worshipper.

I have heard that for a whole week no wayfarer had come to claim the hospitality of the Friend of God (*Abraham*).

From a cheerful habit he would not eat his morning meal unless some necessitous traveller arrived on his journey.

He went out and looked out on every side, and surveyed every point of the valley.

He saw only, like a reed in the desert, one solitary man, whose hair was white with the snows of age.

He addressed him with a courteous welcome, and gave him an invitation after the custom of the liberal:

"O dear to me as the apple of mine eye, do me the kindness to eat of my bread and of my salt."

Gladly he assented, leaped up, and quickened his step, for he knew the character of the inviter: on whom be peace!

They who ministered to the hospitality of the Friend of God seated the poor old man in the seat of honour.

He commanded and they prepared the table, and his companions placed themselves around it;

But when the company began—" In the name of God"—no voice from the old man reached the ear.

Then he said:—" O thou that hast seen many days, I perceive that thou art not pious and earnest as an old man should be.

Is it not proper, when thou eatest thy daily bread, to name the name of the Lord who gave it ?"

He replied :—" I have not followed thy way, for I was never taught it by the Priest of the Fire-worshippers."

Then the Prophet of good omen knew that the old man was an Infidel, doomed to perdition ;

And when he found him to be an alien, he assailed him with contumelies as a wicked wretch too unholy to consort with the Holy.

Then came an Angel from the Creator who reproved him sternly, saying,—

" I have bestowed upon him life and daily food for a hundred years, and is he become to thee an abomination in a single day ?

If he hath offered up his adoration before Fire, art thou therefore to withdraw from him the hand of benevolence ?"—*Graf's Text p.* 142. *Transl. I.* 99.

The Wise-man and the Cheat.

An eloquent fellow came to a Wise-man, saying— "I am broken-down and stuck fast, entangled in the clay.

I am indebted to one of the base-born rabble ten dirams, the weight of which lieth on my breast like ten hundred-weights.

All night he maketh my condition miserable; all day he followeth my tail like my shadow.

He hath sorely broken my heart with his words; my inmost soul as the door of my house.

He talketh as though God, since his mother bore him, had never given him aught save those ten dirams.

Of the books of his religion he knoweth not the first letter, and can recite only the chapter of denial.

Not a day doth the sun rise above the mountain, that this wretched man is not battering my door with the knocker.

I am thinking whether some generous man will not aid me with silver to lift this stone from my breast!"

The old man, endowed with a happy disposition,

listened to these words, and straightway placed two coins within his sleeve.

The gold fell like a fairy-gift into his hand, and off he went with a face as bright as the gold.

"Shaikh," said some one to him, "thou knowest not what that man is! When that man dieth there will be no weeping over him.

A beggar! who could put a saddle on a male lion, and place his Vizier and his Horseman as cleverly as Alu Zaaid." (*Note* 3.)

The holy man looked at him displeased, and exclaimed—"Thou who art not a man with a tongue, incline to me thine ear a moment.

If that, which I deemed him to be, is right, I have saved his reputation in the face of the people ;

And if he be but an impudent pretender, why, then—he hath played me a trick! as thou hast suspected."—*Graf's Text p.* 144. *Trans. I.* 100.

The True Works of Piety.

I have heard that an old man on a pilgrimage to the Holy-place, at each step made two head-bowings in prayer.

So warmly was he pursuing his path towards God, that he paused not to pluck out a thorn from his foot.

At last, through the temptations of his treacherous heart, his acts appeared so praiseworthy in his own sight,

That through the machinations of the Evil One he was well nigh falling into the pit,

Persuading himself that he could not by possibility walk on any road preferable to this ;

And had the mercy of God not intervened, his vain-glory would have hurried him on to destruction;

But his good genius in an inaudible voice whispered to him—" O happy and fortune-favoured man,

Think not, that because thou hast discharged a service of prayer, thou hast brought into this Court a graceful free-will offering ;

To give peace to a single heart by a kindly act is worth more than a thousand head-bowings in prayer!

—*Graf's Text p.* 151. *Transl. I.* 105.

Humanity.

A man found in the desert a thirsty dog, which from want of drink was at its last gasp.

The worthy man made a bucket of his cap, and twisted his muslin sash into a rope.

Then he girded his waist and extended his arms for service, and gave to the feeble dog a sup of water.

The Prophet revealed of his future condition, that the Supreme Judge had for this act pardoned his sins.

Oh! if thou hast been a hard man, bethink thee; learn to be kind, and make beneficence thy business!

If a kindness done to a dog is not lost, how should that be which is done to a worthy man?

Do good as you find it offered to your hand: the Master of the Universe hath closed against no one the door for doing some good.

To give from your treasury a talent of gold is of less worth than a carat bestowed by the hand of labour.

Each one shall bear the burthen proportioned to his strength: the foot of a locust would be heavy for an ant.—*Graf's Text p.* 156. *Trans. I.* 109.

The Hard-hearted Man Punished.

Thou who hast been blessed with the gifts of fortune, be gentle with the people, that God may not to-morrow deal harshly with thee.

Hath one fallen down he will not always be perplexed, for there is ever one at hand to take the hand of the fallen.

Beware that thou command not thy slave cruelly, for may be hereafter he may become thy commander.

Since dignity and power are not held in perpetuity, use thou no violence with the poor and feeble;

For it may be that he may be raised to rank and authority, as the Pawn at chess may become suddenly Vizier.

Listen then thou far-sighted man to good council; scatter not over hearts the seed of malevolence.

The lord of the harvest injureth himself if he dealeth with the gleaner in a churlish spirit.

Let not him fear who giveth of his wealth to the poor, but him who layeth one man's burthen of grief on the heart of another.

Many a mighty one hath fallen in the course, and to many a one who hath fallen, hath Fortune held out a helping hand.

Beware that thou break not the heart of thy dependents, lest one day thou become thyself dependent on others.

A poor man who hath fallen into a sad condition was complaining one day to a crabbed rich man.

The sour-hearted man gave him of money not a mite, but loaded him in his anger with loud imprecations.

The heart of the beggar was turned to gall by his violence: he lifted up his head in passion and excitement, and exclaimed—"Is it not wonderful!

Wherefore, O God, is the rich man so sour-faced? Perchance he knoweth nothing of the bitterness of begging!"

Short-sighted man he commanded a slave to drive him by main force contumeliously from his gate.

I have heard that through his ingratitude to the All-provider, Fortune at last turned away and deserted him.

His greatness laid down its head amidst ruins, and Mercury dipped his pen in blackness.

Misery left him naked and thin as his shoe-latchet;

nor freed him from his burthen, nor left him aught to bear it.

Fate threw the dust of poverty on his head, and, like a juggler with his cup and ball, left him empty in purse and hand.

His condition was altered from head to foot, and in the course of events Fortune abandoned him.

His servant passed into the hands of a liberal master, large of heart and hand, and of a generous nature.

At the sight of one poor and troubled in circumstances he would be as overjoyed as the needy with his gift.

One evening there came to his door one begging for a morsel, dragging along a body weakened by suffering.

The master thereupon made a sign to his slave, and commanded him to administer solace to the needy one.

The slave carried him a portion from the table, but when he came near him, uttered a distracted cry,

And came back to the merchant with a broken heart and eyes bathed in tears at the strange mystery.

The good-natured master asked him immediately— "What suffering hast thou that thy face is wet with tears?"

He replied—"My breast hath been sadly disturbed by the shattered fortunes of this poor old man.

Once in times past I was his Mamluk (*white slave*) ; then he was master of lands and chattels and silver:

Now his hand is cut short of grandeur and pride, and is held out to beg alms from door to door."

The merchant laughed, and said—"My boy, in this hath been done no wrong. The revolution of the spheres doth injustice to no one !

Is not this man the churlish merchant who in his pride exalted his head to the skies ?

I am the man whom one day he thrust from his door. Now is my day, and the circling universe hath placed him now where I once was.

Heaven again looked down on me with favour, and wiped from my face the dust of affliction.

If God in his wisdom shutteth one door, in his beneficence and mercy he openeth another.

Many a needy bankrupt hath again been made full ; many a prosperous state been turned topsy-turvy.—*Graf's Text. p.* 156. *Transl. I.,* 110.

Shabli and the Ant.

Listen to one of the qualities of good men, if thou art thyself a good man, and benevolently-inclined!

Shabli, returning from the shop of a corn-dealer, carried back to his village on his shoulder a sack of wheat.

He looked, and beheld in that heap of grain an ant which kept running bewildered from corner to corner.

Filled with pity thereat, and unable to sleep at night, he carried it back to its own dwelling, saying— " It were no benevolence to wound and distract this poor ant by severing it from its own place !"

Soothe to rest the hearts of the distracted, wouldest thou be at rest thyself from the blows of fortune !

How sweet are the words of the noble Firdusi, upon whose grave be the mercy of the Benignant One !

" Crush not yonder emmet as it draggeth along its grain ; for it too liveth, and its life is sweet to it."

A shadow must there be, and a stone upon that heart, that could wish to sorrow the heart even of an emmet !

Strike not with the hand of violence the head of the feeble ; for one day, like the ant, thou mayest fall under the foot thyself!

Pity the poor moth in the flame of the taper ; see how it is scorched in the face of the assembly!

Let me remind thee, that if there be many who are weaker than thou art, there may come at last one who is stronger than thou.—*Graf's Text, p.* 160. *Transl. I.,* 113.

Live not on the Labour of others.

A man observed one day a fox without foot or leg, and was perplexed as to the kindness and goodness of God.

How will it be able to prolong its existence? how without leg or claw obtain wherewith to eat?

With this the Derwish was sorely disturbed, but just then came up a lion with a jackal in its jaws.

The lion devoured the unfortunate jackal, but left enough to fill the maw of the fox.

The next day by good chance fell a falcon beside him, so that each day as it came brought sufficient for the day.

The assurance of the eye brought the man a new light, and he went away determined to rely on his Creator only;

And thenceforth to sit down like an ant in its cell, "since not even the elephant can get food by mere force."

So he rested his chin within his collar, saying—" A messenger will be sent me by the All-giver from the unseen world."

But neither stranger nor friend came to minister to his wants, till veins and bone and skin became hard as a claw.

When reason and patience were exhausted through weakness, from the wall of his chamber came a voice to his ear—

"Uprouse thee, lazy man, like a ravening lion; cast not thyself down like a paralyzed fox.

Put forth thy strength like a lion, that something may be left; not like the fox, feed on the lion's leavings!"

He who like a lion is robust and active, if he lie down like a fox is no better than a dog.

Get with thine own hand, and bestow on others, and strive not to live on another's redundancies!

Eat so long as thou canst by the power of thine own arm, for the fruit of thine efforts will be weighed in thine own scales.

Labour like a man, and be ready in doing kindnesses; he is a good-for-nothing fellow who eateth by the toil of another's hand.

Take thou, young man, the hand of the poor man; but throw not thyself on others, saying—"Take *me* by the hand!"

The mercy of God be upon that servant, whose

existence hath been the means of comforting his fellow-creatures !

He may look cheerfully for the good of both dwellings, who hath himself brought good to the people of God.—*Graf's Text, p.* 163. *Transl. I.,* 115.

FROM BOOK THE THIRD:

OF LOVE.

Happy those who are disquieted with anxiety about HIM, if the wound and the balsam are received together!

Scared away from sovereignty, they appear only as beggars; but, in their begging, they are patient through hope.

Every moment they are drinking the water of affliction; but, if it taste bitter, they breathe not a complaint.

In the pleasures of wine there is the pain of the after-headache, and the branch of the rose is armed with its thorn;

But patience is not bitter in memory of the dear one, for even wormwood is sugar from the hand of a friend.

Whom HE hath taken captive, he desireth not

liberty, and the entangled in His noose wisheth not for deliverance.

Beggars though they live, they are kings in their isolation; though their guides have lost their track, they still look towards the resting places.

Intoxicated with passion they mind not reproach, as the inebriated camel beareth its burden more lightly.

How should the multitude find its way to their secret chambers, for, like the waters of life, they are hidden in darkness.

They kindle themselves the flame, which as a moth consumeth them; not wrapping themselves up like the silkworm in its own web.

Seeking for the soul's repose on the bosom which only can give repose, their lips are still dry with thirst on the very margin of the stream.

Not that they have no power to drink the water, but that their thirst could not be quenched even on the banks of the Nile.—*Graf's Text, p.* 191. *Trans. I.,* 139.

Humility.—The Glowworm.

Perchance thou mayest have seen in the garden, or on the foot of a hillock, a small worm, which in the night shineth like a lamp.

Some one said to it—" O night-illuminating worm, what becometh of thee that thou never comest out during the day?"

Hear what that little earth-born fiery worm replied:—

" In the day, as in the night, I am equally in the field; but I veil my lustre in the presence of the sun."—*Graf's Text, p.* 217.   *Transl. I.,* 161.

The Unjustly Punished.

During a tumult in one of the towns of Syria, they arrested an old man of a happy disposition.

Even now his words are in my ear, whilst they were binding him hand and foot,—

" If the Sultan hath not given his authority, to whom belongeth the power of subjecting me to this violence ?

It may be right, that I should hold even an enemy for a friend, if I know that a friend hath sent him to me.

Whether it be grandeur and dignity, whether it be degradation and chains, I know, that it cometh from God, not from Omar or Zaid (*not from this man or that*).

If thou art a wise man fear not the malady, and take, however bitter it may be, whatever medicine the physician sendeth thee.

Swallow whatever cometh through the hand of a friend: the sick man is not more learned than the doctor.—*Graf's Text, p.* 217. *Transl. I.,* 162.

The Moth and the Taper.

Some one said to the moth—"My worthy friend, go, chuse for thy friend one suitable to thy condition.

Go thy way by the path which leadeth towards hope : whither will the love of the taper conduct thee ?

Thou art no salamander, circle not round the flame; in the battle-field is needed the strength of a hero.

The blind mole lieth concealed from the sun ; it is mere folly to use thy palm against an arm of iron !

The man whom thou knoweth to be thine enemy, there is no wisdom in taking for a friend !

No one will say to thee, thou doest well to hazard thy life in his affairs.

The beggar who should demand the daughter of a king would only draw blows upon himself, and nurse a vain ambition.

How could she take such a one as thee for a lover, upon whose countenance rest the looks of kings and sultans ?

Think not, that in that splendid circle a centre could be found for a bankrupt like thee !

And however gentle she may be with the people, thinkest thou that she could show any warmth towards one so helpless as thou art?"

See what that flame-loving moth replied:—" Why wonder?—though I be burnt by it, I fear it not.

My fire, like that of the friend of God, is in my heart; the flame, believe me, is a bed of roses.

Neither of my own free will cast I myself into the fire; for the chain of affection was laid upon my neck.

I was still at a distance when it began to glow, nor is this the moment that it was lighted-up within me.

Who shall impute it to me as a fault, that I am enchanted by my friend, that I am content in casting myself at his feet?

Knowest thou wherefore I am eager to perish?—If He *is*, though I am *not*, it is all right!

Why repeat to me:—" Chuse a friend who is suitable to thyself; one who is able to sympathize with thee in thy sorrows?

Advice to me in so distracted a condition is as though thou shouldest say to a scorpion-bitten man: " Do not complain!"

Offer not counsel, wondering man! to any one, when thou knowest he will not receive it.

To the helpless man whose bridle hath slipped from his hand will they say:—"Push on thy horse gently, my boy?"

It is good, O my son, the saying of Sindbad:— "Love is the fire, advice is the wind."

By wind the hot fire becometh only the hotter; by wounds the tiger becometh only the more savage.

When I looked upon thee as good, I see thee committing evil; how should I go after thee, when I see thee devoted only to thyself?

Seek something better than thyself, and count it a gain, for with one like thyself it is but time lost.

Only self-worshippers follow those like themselves, as the intoxicated rush towards the dangerous quarter.

As soon as I engaged myself in this affair, at once I staked my head against my heart (*my affections*) in its pursuit.

Whoever is sincere in his devotion, will expose his life; whoever is timid is but a lover of himself.

Death on a sudden draweth me into his ambush; how much better that I fall into the snares of my beloved one!

Since without doubt death is written on my brow, death will be sweeter by the hand of the comforter.

Wilt thou not one day helplessly surrender thy soul? Better then is it that thou shouldst surrender it at the feet of one who loveth thee."—*Graf's Text, p.* 224. *Transl. I.,* 166.

The same subject.

I remember, that one night, when I could not close my eyes in sleep, I heard the moth say to the taper :

"I am a lover, therefore it is right that I should be burnt; but wherefore should'st thou be lamenting and shedding tears ?"

It replied : O my poor airy friend, my honey-sweet Shirin is going away;

And since my Shirin hath left me, like Ferhâd's, my head is all on fire."

So spake the taper, and each moment a flood of sorrow flowed down over its pale cheek.

Then it continued : "O pretender, love is no affair of thine; for thou hast neither patience nor persistency.

Thou takest to flight before a slight flame ; I stand firm till I am totally consumed.

Thou mayest just singe a wing at the fire of love ; look at me who burn from head to foot."

A part of the night was not yet gone, when suddenly a Peri-faced damsel extinguished the light.

Then said the taper : "My breath is departed, the smoke is over my head ; such, my son, is the ending of love !"

If thou would'st learn the moral of the story, it is this : Only will the pangs of burning affection cease, when life's taper is extinct.

Weep not over this monument of thy perished friend! rather praise Allah, that he is accepted by him.

If thou art indeed a lover, wash not the pains of love from thine head; wash rather, like Sadi, thine hand from all malevolence.

The man who volunteereth a service of peril will not withdraw his grasp from his purpose, though stones and arrows rain down upon his head.

I have said to thee: " Take heed how thou goest to the sea ! but if thou wilt go resign thyself to its billows."—*Graf's Text, p.* 228. *Transl. I.*, 169.

FROM THE FOURTH BOOK.
ON HUMILITY.

The Holy-One, the Lord, created thee of clay; therefore, O servant, prostrate thyself as the earth!

Be not thou covetous, arrogant, a world-spoiler; thou art formed of the clay, resemble not fire.

Whilst the fire exalteth its neck proudly and terribly, the clay lieth prostrate in the consciousness of its helplessness.

Whilst that displayeth its haughtiness, this exhibiteth its littleness; of that were created Demons, of this was formed Man!

A drop of rain trickled from a cloud into the ocean. When it beheld the breadth of its waters, it was utterly confounded.

"What a place this sea is! and what am I! If it is existent, verily I am non-existent."

Whilst it was thus regarding itself with the eye of

contempt, an oyster received and cherished it in its bosom.

Fortune preferred it to a place of honour; for it became a renowned royal pearl.

Because it was humble, it found exaltation; it knocked at the door of nonentity, that it might arise into being.—*Graf's Text, p.* 230. *Transl. I.*, 171.

Humility.

A youth, intelligent and of a good disposition, arrived by sea at a Grecian port.

They perceived that he was endowed with excellence, and judgment, and an inclination to asceticism, and placed him accordingly in a sacred building.

The Head of the devotees said to him one day: " Go and cast out the dirt and the rubbish from the Mosque."

As soon as the young traveller heard the words he went forth, but no one discovered any sign of his return.

The Superior and the brethren laid a charge against him, saying: "This young devotee hath no aptness for his vocation."

The following day one of the society met him in the road and said to him: " Thou hast shewed an unseemly and perverse disposition.

Didst thou not know, O self-opinionated boy, that it is through obedience men attain to honour?"

He began to weep, and replied: " O friend of my

soul, and enlightener of my heart, it is in earnestness and in sincerity that I have acted thus.

I found in that sacred building neither dust nor defilement: only myself was polluted in that holy place.

Therefore, immediately I drew back my foot, feeling that to withdraw *myself* was to cleanse the Mosque from dirt and rubbish."

For the devotee there is only one path: to submit his body to humiliation.

Thine exaltation must come from choosing self-abasement: to reach the lofty roof there is no ladder save this.—*Graf's Text, p.* 231. *Trans. I.* 172.

The Sinner and Jesus.

One of the narrators hath committed to words that in the time of Jesus, on whom be a blessing!

Was one of the dissolute, who had consumed his all, and reached the utmost bounds of error and folly.

Bold, hard-hearted, and of blackened name, Eblis (*Satan*) himself would have been ashamed of his impurity.

He had spent all his days to no profit; never tried to soothe the heart of any one.

His brain was emptied of understanding, and filled with arrogance, and his body was fat with forbidden morsels.

The skirts of his garment were stained with iniquity; begrimed like a smoky dwelling with shamelessness;

His feet not rightly directed, like those of the clear-sighted; his ear not one disposed to listen to good counsel.

Men held him in abomination like the year of famine, pointing to him from afar, as one pointeth to the new moon.

A scorching wind had burnt up his harvest, and he had not picked up a single wholesome grain.

He had run the black-book so completely through and through, that there remained no longer a page to write on.

Sinful and wilful and devoted to his pleasures, night and day he passed carelessly in drunkenness and revelling.

I have heard that Jesus returning from the desert was passing by the hermitage of a Devotee.

The Anchorite came down from his private cell, and fell at his feet with his head on the ground.

The Sinner at last approached them from a distance, dazzled at their presence like the moth before the candle, gazing upon them earnestly, sighing and bashful, like a poor man in the presence of a wealthy merchant.

Silent and motionless, burning pleas upon his lips, for nights spent till daylight in careless negligence,

Raining tears of sorrow from his eyes as from a cloud, that life had been passed, alas! in so much heedlessness.

"I have thrown away the ready money of my precious life, and have brought to my account no act of goodness!

Let no living man be ever like me, for to him to die were far better than to live!

He hath escaped well who died in infancy; who hath not, an old man, had to bear the burthen of shame!

Forgive, O Creator of the World, my offences; for if they rise with me they will be but sad companions!"

In such tones lamenting stood the Ancient Sinner, imploring help from Him who is the Helper;

Hanging down his head for very shame, and a river of tears flowing upon his bosom.

Meanwhile, the Devotee, half turning away, his brain puffed up with vain self-esteem, fixed a sour brow on the wicked one, and exclaimed,

"Why doth this ruined fellow follow our steps?— ignorant and ill-omened claim kindred with us?

Encompassed with fire up to the very neck—his life given over to the storm of the passions,

What good can come from his polluted breath? What right can such as he have to seek the society of the Messiah and me?

What was he that he should press his companionship on us? Rather let him follow his own deeds to Hell!

I am pained at the very aspect of his ugly countenance! May it never be that I should fall into his fire!

At the resurrection, when all men are assembled for judgment, let not my resurrection, O God, be with his!

At this moment an inspired voice from the august Lord of all Perfection came to Jesus, on whom be blessings!

"Though this be a wise man and that be a fool, the invocation of each will be accepted by me.

The one who turned his bright day to corruption hath lamented it to me with burning tears.

Whosoever cometh to seek me in his helplessness, him will I in no wise drive away from the threshold of mercy;

His evil works will I remove from him, and for what he hath done of good I will bring him to Paradise."

And if he who hath been the Devotee of holiness scorneth to sit beside him in eternity,

Say to him, "Fear not, that he should disgrace thee in the resurrection; for this one shall they bear to Paradise and that one to the fire.

He knew not that in the Court of Heaven helplessness is esteemed more highly than self-exaltation.

If thy garments be clean and thine actions be foul, thou needest no key to the door of Hell.

At that threshhold weakness and misery avail more than worship and presumption."

If thou numberest thyself amongst the good thou art evil; self-estimation is not amongst the things which belong to godliness!

If thou art a man, speak not much about thine own manliness; for not every champion driveth the ball to the goal.

He is but a simpleton who, because the onion hath a perfect rind, thinketh that it is a pestachio nut, and hath within it a kernel.

Devotion of this kind bringeth with it no good! go, ask forgiveness rather for lack of devotion!

That senseless man will gain nothing from his worship, who, good in his own esteem, thinketh evil of others.

Words are what is left as the memorials of the wise; retain in thy memory one word of Sadi's:

" Better is the Sinner who hath thoughts about God than the Saint who hath only the show of sanctity!"—*Graf's Text, p.* 234.   *Transl. I.* 175.

FROM THE FIFTH BOOK.
ON SUBMISSION TO GOOD COUNSEL.

One night I was burning the oil of reflection and was kindling the lamp of eloquence,

When an idle chatterer heard me reciting; one who see'th no path but that of detraction.

Though obliged to commend, yet he found such a variety of blemishes in the pages that he was constrained by the pain to cry out against them.

"Yes, his thoughts are eloquent and his counsels exalted, and he is elegant enough about temperance, fine sentiment, and good advice;

But he hath nothing to say on javelin, mace, and heavy battle-axe; elegancies of this kind he must leave to others."

He knew not that my intention is not to speak

of war; but were it so, my majesty of diction is not scanty.

I am able enough to wield the sword of the tongue, and in one moment could utterly confound his very being.

Let him come, and let us do battle in *this* kind of elegance, and our foe shall rest his head on a stone, not a cushion.—*Graf's Text, p.* 286. *Transl. II.* 1.

The Camel and her Foal.

A camel's foal said to her mother: "After journey-ing so long rest for awhile."

She replied: "Were the rein in my hand, no one would behold me conveying this burthen in the file."

Fate beareth onward the ship whither it will, how-soever the master may rend the clothes on his body.

Fix not thine eye, O Sadi, on the hand of any one; the All-giver will be thy provider, and that is enough!

If thou reverest God, he sufficeth thee; and if He rejecteth thee, no one else will receive thee.

If He deigneth to crown thee lift up thy head; but if not, sink it in hopelessness.—*Graf's Text, p.* 301. *Transl. II.* 12.

FROM THE SIXTH BOOK:
ON CONTENTMENT.

He hath never known God, or offered real worship, who is not contented with his state and daily bread.

Contentment is the gain which maketh man truly rich; make this well known to those who covet the riches of the world!

Try to win quietude, thou restless man; for on a rolling stone groweth no verdure.

Nourish not the body, if thou bee'st a man of intelligence and wisdom; for whilst thou thinkest thou art feeding, thou art killing it.

Men of understanding nourish the virtues; those who nourish the body are starvers of the spirit.

Eating and sleeping are the track which the beasts pursue; to follow their track is the way of the uninstructed.

Whoso first silenced the hound of greediness, he it was who taught man to listen to morality.

Favoured indeed by Fortune is the recluse who can draw in his cell his nourishment from knowledge.

For those to whom the walking in the truth is clear will not make choice of that which is false.

But if they cannot discern between light and darkness, what mattereth to them the aspect of a Demon, or the cheek of a Houri.

It is thou who hast cast thyself into the well, because thou didst not distinguish the well from the highway.

When the male-falcon is soaring to the pinnacle of heaven how could it do so were the stone of avidity attached to its pinions.

But if he can free his skirt from the grasp of sensuality, he may reach the Sidrah-tree itself.

If thou wilt control thine appetites, and eat less than thy want, thou mayest assume to thyself the nature of angels.

How should the savage-lion become an angel? It is impossible to fly to heaven out of the mud;

Thou must apprentice thyself to human habits; then mayst thou think of those which are angelic!

If thou art mounted with girded loins on an ungovernable colt, look well that it free not its head from thy grasp;

For if it once pluck the bridle from thine hand, it will kill itself, and spill thine own blood.—*Graf's Text. p.* 308. *Transl. II.* 18.

The Father and his Infant.

An infant had arrived at the time of teething. The father sank his head on his breast, exclaiming,

"Whence shall I bring him bread and food? and humanity will not permit me to leave him without."

Whilst he was talking thus despairingly to his wife, hear the manly way in which the woman replied.

" Let not Iblis (*Satan)* fright thee with thoughts that he must die. The same one who gave him teeth, will give him bread also.

The Lord of Day hath surely power enough to provide him his daily food : be not disquieted !

He who formed the child in the womb, will also prescribe for his life and nourishment.

The master who hath purchased a slave will provide—how should it be otherwise!—that which will support the slave.

Hast thou not so much reliance on Him, the Creator, as the slave hath upon his master?"—*Graf's Text, p.* 319. *Transl. II.* 27.

Be Prepared for Vicissitudes.

The vineyard doth not perpetually produce the moist cluster of grapes; sometimes it yieldeth its fruit, and sometimes it scattereth its leaves.

Great men, like the sun, are veiled in mist; the envious, like burning charcoal, are extinguished in the water.

The sun gradually cometh forth again from under the cloud; the charcoal dieth in the water for ever.

Fear not, my valued friend, fear not obscurity, for not unfrequently lieth hid within it the fountain of life.

Doth not the earth find rest again after the earthquake? By your painful journey, did you not obtain what you were in want of?

In disappointment consume not thy soul with anxiety; the night, O my brother, is big with the day.—*Graf's Text, p.* 325. *Transl. II.* 33.

FROM THE SEVENTH BOOK OF THE BOSTAN.

My theme is rectitude, and self-government, and good habits, not the practising-ground, and horsemen, and mace, and ball.

Thine enemy is the spirit which dwelleth with thyself; why seek in a stranger one to contend with ?

He who can bridle his spirit from that which is forbidden hath surpassed Rustam and Sâm in valour.

Chastise thou thyself like a child with thine own rod, and brain not others with thy ponderous mace.

An enemy will suffer no harm from one like thee, unless thou art able to overcome thyself.

Thy body is a city full of good and evil; thou art the Sultan, and reason thy wise Vizier.

Like base-coin men whose heads are exalted, live in this city Pride, and Sensuality, and fierce Passions;

Contentment, Conscientiousness, those of good name, lovely as Houris; Lust and Ambition, Robbery and Treachery.

When the Sultan maketh the bad his familiars, where can the prudent find a place of rest?

Appetite, and greediness, and pride, and envy, cleave to thyself as the blood in thy veins, and the soul in thy vitals.

If these enemies have once obtained the mastery of thee, they rush out and will overpower all thy discretion.

There need be no contest with appetite and passion, if so be that Reason hold out a sharp claw.

The Chief who knoweth not how to manage his enemy will hardly save his chieftainship from his enemy's hand.

What need can there be in this book to say much : a little is enough for him who goeth right to his mark. *Graf's Text, p.* 326. *Transl. II.* 34.

Keep your own Secret.

Sultan Takish once committed a secret to his slaves, which they were enjoined to tell again to no one.

For a year it had not passed from his breast to his lips; it was published to all the world in a single day.

He commanded the executioner to sever with the sword their heads from their bodies without mercy.

One from their midst exclaimed,—"Beware! slay not the slaves, for the fault is thine own.

Why didst thou not dam up at once what at first was but a fountain?—What availeth it to do so, when it is become a torrent?"

Take heed, that thou reveal not to any one the secret of thy heart, for he will divulge it to all the world.

Thy jewels thou may'st consign to the keeping of thy treasurer; but thy secret reserve for thine own keeping.

Whilst thou utterest not a word, thou hast thine hand upon it; when thou hast uttered it, it hath laid its hand upon thee.

Thou knowest, that when the demon hath escaped from his cage, by no "adjuration" will he enter it again.

The word is an enchained Demon in the pit of the heart, let it not escape to the tongue and the palate.

It is possible to open a way to the strong Demon; to retake him by stratagem is not possible.

A child may untether "Lightning" (*the Hero Rustams' war-horse*), but a hundred Rustams will not bring him to the halter again.

Take heed, that thou say not that which, if it come to the crowd, may bring trouble to a single individual.

It was well said by his wife to an ignorant peasant,— "Either talk sensibly or hold thy tongue."—*Graf's Text, p.* 329. *Transl. II.* 37.

Speech and Silence.

A man in Cairo of fair mien but clothed in rags maintained for some time great silence.

Intelligent men from far and near circled round him, as the light-loving moth about the taper.

One night communing with his heart he said within himself :—" The man lieth concealed beneath his tongue.

If I thus keep my head hid in my breast, how should men know, how learned I am ! "

So he spake out his words, and enemy and friend discovered at once, that there was not a more ignorant fellow in Cairo.

Respect for him gone, and, matters looking badly, he set off on his travels, and wrote on an arch of a mosque,

" If I had looked at myself in the mirror, I should not in mine ignorance have rent my veil.

I came out from that veil so ugly, because I fancied that I was so handsome."

The man of few words hath loud voices in his

favour; when thou hast spoken, and thy brilliance is departed, hie thee away!

To thee who art master of thy reason, silence is a mark of calmness; to the incapable, a veil to cover him.

If thou art a wise man, destroy not reverence; and if thou art ignorant, rend not the veil which hideth thee.

The thought of thine heart be not hasty to reveal; for thou wilt be able to show it, whensoever thou mayest wish;

But when a man's secret is once made public, no effort will avail to conceal it again.

The beasts are silent, and man is gifted with the faculty of speech; but a man who talketh at random is worse than the beasts.

When a man uttereth his words, he should do it with understanding; if not, like the beasts, he had better hold his peace.

He who is born of man is distinguished by articulation and reason; let him not show his folly by chattering like a parrot. — *Graf's Text*, *p*. 331. *Transl. II.* 38.

Calumny worse than Theft.

Some one said to me—I took it for a pleasantry—that Thieving was a less unrighteous thing than Calumny.

I replied, " O my friend, thine head is distracted: thy words come to mine ears with amazement.

What of better dost thou see in robbery, that thou exaltest such villany above calumny ? " " Yes, he answered, " Robbers exhibit deeds of daring : they fill their bellies by the strong hand.

What seeketh the simpleton to gain by calumny ?— He hath smeared the page, and got nothing to eat by it."—*Graf's Text, p.* 341. *Transl. II.* 46.

How to bring up a Son.

When thy son hath passed his tenth year, say to him,—"Sit apart from strangers."

It is not well to kindle a fire near cotton, for whilst thou closest thine eyes thy house may be burning.

If thou desirest that thy name should remain in its place, teach thy son understanding and knowledge.

If he possess not wisdom and knowledge, thou wilt die, and no one will remain after thee.

Oft-times hath the son-had to bear hardships in the end, when he hath been too tenderly nurtured by his father.

Keep him within bounds of prudence and moderation; if thou holdest him dear, indulge him not in delicacies.

In his childhood thou must give him chastisement and instruction; must teach the good and the evil by threats and by promises.

To the young learner praise, and commendation, and "well-done!" are better than chiding and frightening in the master.

Teach to thy pupil some kind of handicraft, hast thou in thy hand all the wealth of Karun;

For what knowest thou, whether some shift of fortune will not turn him out of his home to a distant land?

Place no reliance on present prosperity, for thy wealth may no longer remain in thine hand.

Let his hand be but skilful at some trade, and why should he stretch out the hand of necessity to any one;

Thy purse of silver and gold may come to an end; the purse of the artizan will never be empty.

Dost thou not know how Sadi attained his wishes?

He roamed not over plains, nor divided seas:

In his youth he bore cuffs from his elders, and in his age God gave him recreation.

Whoever submitteth his neck to authority, doth it not frequently happen that he cometh to authority himself?

The child who hath never felt the austerity of the teacher, will have to learn from the severity of life.

Be good to the child, and treat him with kindness, that his eye may not be directed to look for it from others.

Whoever doth not himself sympathize with his

child, will make others sympathize, and gain him a bad name.

Take heed, that thou commit him not to a vicious teacher, for he will make him as vicious and led-astray as himself.

Thou canst not find him a blacker book than that good-for-nothing fellow, to blacken him ere his face is blackened by his beard.

Fly from that man so lost to honour, that his unworthiness causeth worthy men to weep.

If his son hath sat in the society of Kalanders, say to his father, "Hope no good of him.

Cry not—'Alas!' over his death or ruin; for it is well that the degenerate one should die before his father."—*Graf's Text, p.* 354.   *Transl. II.* 59.

FROM BOOK THE EIGHTH:
ON THANKFULNESS.

I cannot draw a breath without gratitude to the Friend, though I know no gratitude which is worthy of him!

Every hair of my body is a gift from Him; how express my gratitude for every hair!

Praise be to the Lord, the giver of all good, who created his slave out of nonentity!

Who is there who hath power to describe His beneficence; for the description of His favours would quite overwhelm him!

The Wonderful One! Who created man out of clay; and gave him a soul, and understanding, and wisdom, and a heart!

From the loins of thy father till thine hoary head, see what honour He bestoweth on thee from the unseen world!

Since He created thee holy, be thou wise and holy ; for it is shameful to return impure to the earth.

Gradually disperse the dust from the mirror, for it will not take the polish when the rust hath eaten into it.

Wast thou not in the beginning but a drop of water? Now that thou art a man expel from thine head every grain of egotism.

When thou hast gained thy daily bread by thine own endeavours, place not thy reliance on the strength of thine own arm!

Wherefore discernest thou not God, O thou worshipper of self, who gave to thine hand and arm its activity?

When from thy labouring thou receivest any thing, know that it is by the grace of God, not by thine own efforts.

No one by the power of his wrist drove the ball to the goal; render the praise to Him, the All-gracious!

Thou art not able to stand, or set one foot before another, did not assistance come to thee every moment from the unseen world!—*Graf's Text, p.* 371. *Transl. II.* 73.

King Toghrul and the Sentinel.

I have heard that King Toghrul came in his rounds on a Hindu sentinel.

The snow was falling thick, and it rained in torrents, and he shivered with the cold like the star Canopus.

The heart of the king was moved with compassion, and he said,—" Thou shalt put on my fur-mantle ;

Wait a moment at the end of the terrace, and I will send it out by the hand of a slave."

Meanwhile a piercing wind was blowing, and the king walked into his royal hall.

There the sight of a lovely lady so enchanted him, that the poor sentinel entirely slipped his memory.

As though the wintry cold were not suffering enough, to his evil fortune were added the pangs of disappointment.

Hear, whilst the king slept in comfort, what the watchman was saying towards the dawning of the morning.

" Perhaps thy good fortune made thee forgetful, for thy hand was clasped in the hand of thy beloved.

For thee the night passed in mirth and enjoyment; what knowest thou of how it passed with us?

When the company of the caravan are stooping the head over the platter, what concern have they for those who have fallen down in the sand (*desert* ?)

O boatman, launch thy boat into the water, for it hath nearly reached the head of the helpless waders!

Stay your steps awhile, ye active youths, for in the caravan are weak old men also!

Thou who art sleeping sweetly in thy litter, whilst the bridle of the camel is in the hand of the driver,

What to thee is plain, and hill, and stone, and sand!—Ask, how it is with those who are left behind on the journey!

Thou who art borne along on thy high and strong dromedary, how knowest thou how he fareth who is travelling on foot!

They who in the quiet of their hearts are reposing at the resting-place, what know they of the condition of the hungry wayfarer!"—*Graf's Text*, *p.* 381. *Transl. II.* 81.

FROM THE NINTH BOOK:
ON CONVERSION.

Come thou whose life hath reached its seventieth year!—perchance thou hast been asleep, and it is gone to the wind.

Thou hast made ample provision for thy living; what preparation hast thou made for thy departure?

At the resurrection, when the market of heaven is thrown open, good works are the price which must be paid for the pleasant mansions.

Whatever capital thou bringest, so much wilt thou carrry back; and if thou art bankrupt, thou canst purchase naught but shame:

For by how much the market is more abundantly supplied with wares, by so much will the empty-handed be grieved in his heart.

If out of fifty dirhams thou losest five, from the loss of those five thine heart is afflicted :

If fifty years have slipped from thy grasp, the five days which remain count as a treasure.

If the poor dead man had but a tongue, with shouts and groans he would cry aloud,

"O thou living-one, to whom speech is still possible, press not thy lips together, rest not, like the dead, from praising God!"

If thou hast passed thy day in carelessness, count at once as thine opportunity the few moments that still are left thee.—*Graf's Text, p.* 398.   *Transl. II.* 97.

The Gold-finder.

A man of unsullied morals and a worshipper of God found by chance a lump of gold.

His once clearly-discerning head was so bewildered by the gain, that his hitherto pure heart became darkened thereby.

All the night long he kept thinking,—"'This wealth and treasure, withersoever we push our journey, will suffer no exhaustion.

Besides, when I am too weak to rise, I shall not have to keep bowing and lifting myself up again to any one.

I will build myself a palace with foundations of marble, the beams of its roof of fresh aloes-wood.

It shall have a private chamber for the entertainment of my friends, the door of which shall open into the palace-garden.

I wore myself down with sewing patch to patch on my garments; envy of others consumed mine eye and my brain.

Now my meat shall be cooked for me by servants, and I will cherish my soul in quietness.

My bed hath been hitherto a hard one and made of felt ; my couch shall henceforth be of the finest tapestry."

The crab so plunged its claws into his brain, that his fancies turned him into dotage and insanity.

Attention to his devotions and duties was forgotten ; and to food, and sleep, and praise, and prayers alike.

He went forth into a solitary place, his head distracted with delusions, for he found no spot in which he could sit down and remain at rest.

There he saw a man who was tempering clay at the head of a grave, and who was making brick of the clay of the grave.

Then the holy man fell into deep thought, and said,—" O short-sighted soul, take council from this :

Why bind thine heart to this brick of gold, when one day they will make bricks of thine own clay ?

Thou careless man, who in thy thought about gain and riches tramplest under foot the capital of life !"

Over our clay will blow a wind so strong, that every atom of it will be borne to a different place.

The dust of ambition hath so choked up the eye of judgment, that the hot-wind of passion hath burnt up the harvest of life.—*Graf's Text, p.* 409. *Transl. II.* 107.

The Two Enemies.

There were two men between whom was enmity, and contention, and who fought like tigers for the pride of being one above the other;

Flying from one another in their aversion to such a degree that the heavens seemed too narrow to contain them.

On the head of one of them Destiny brought down his legion, and his days of delight came to an end.

The other in his evil thoughts was inwardly filled with gladness, and when some time had passed he went to visit his grave.

The chamber of his tomb, which once had been ornamented with gilding like a palace, he found besmeared with clay.

Exultingly he went down to his couch, and said to himself with a laugh on his open lip,

" Joy for the rest of life to him who after the death of his enemy is in the embraces of a friend.

There is no need to weep over the death of that man, who hath lived one day after the death of his enemy."

In the excess of his hatred with the strength of his arm he tore down a board from the face of the sepulchre.

He saw the royal head brought down to a pit; the two eyes, which once looked round upon the world, stuffed with clay;

His person a captive in the prison of the tomb; his body the food of the worm, and the prey of the ant;

From the revolutions of the spheres the full-moon of his countenance dwindled away to the changing moon: from the violence of fate his cypress-like form reduced to a bodkin;

The palm of his hand and the power of his fist disjoined by time, member from member.

Then was his heart so filled with pity, that with his weeping he changed the dust into clay.

He repented himself of what he had done, and of his ugly disposition, and caused to be inscribed on the stone of the sepulchre,

"Make no rejoicing over the death of any one; for thine own time will not be long after his."

An intelligent holy-man heard of this, and breathed out a prayer, saying,—"O all-powerful Creator,

It would be wonderful, wert thou not to extend thy mercy to one over whom his very enemy hath wept with many groans!

May my body also one day be found in such a condition, that the hearts of my enemies may be kindled towards me!

Perhaps the heart of the Friend will have mercy upon me, when he see'th that even my enemies have forgiven me."—*Graf s Text, p.* 411.   *Transl. II.* 108.

Sadi and the Ring.

I recall to my memory, how during the life of my father—may the rain of mercy every moment descend upon him!—

He bought for me in my childhood a tablet and a writing-book, and for my finger a golden seal-ring.

As it happened, a pedlar came to the door, and in exchange for a date carried off the ring from my hand;

For a little child cannot estimate the value of a seal-ring, and will easily part with it for anything sweet.

And thou too dost not estimate the value of a life, who throwest it away in luxurious indulgencies.

In the resurrection, when the righteous arrive at the lofty place, and are raised from the damp pit to the region of the Pleiades,

Will thine head not be bowed down in abasement, when all *thy* works shall be assembled before thee?

O brother, be ashamed now to do the deeds of the bad, that thou mayest not need to be ashamed in the face of the good.

On that day when inquest shall be made into deeds

and words, and the body even of those who have
striven after holiness shall tremble,

With what excuse for thy sins wilt thou hear *thy*
summons, when the very prophets will be over-
whelmed with terror? *Graf's Text, p.* 416. *Transl.*
II. 112.

The Bad Man and the Sheikh.

Knock at the door of mercy, ere the chastisement come; for lamentation is useless when thou art under the rod.

Lift up thine head from the bosom of carelessness for to-morrow shame may no longer remain in thy breast.

A man of an excellent character was passing by one addicted to forbidden things;

Who sat, his face suffused with the dew of shame, and was exclaiming:—" What shame to be seen thus by the Shaikh of my village!"

The holy man heard his words, and approached him, and said with some asperity :

" O young man shouldest thou not be ashamed of thyself, that, when God is present, thou art ashamed at seeing me ?

Feel so much shame in the presence of thy Lord, as thou wouldest feel in that of the faultless and thy friends.

Thou wilt not find rest beside thy fellow-man : go look for it to the side of God, and that will be enough."

—*Graf's Text, p.* 426.   *Transl. II.* 119.

Ask pardon in time.

A king of Damaghan beat some one with a drumstick so soundly, that his cries resounded like his drum.

In the night he was so restless, that he was unable to sleep. A pious man, who was passing, said:

"If thou hadst brought thy regrets to the prince in the evening, thou would'st not have had to bear this humiliation in the morning."

He will not need to be ashamed in the day of judgment, who brings his sorrows at night into the court of the Supreme.

If to-day thou canst hold up thine head in sincerity, what fear that the Merciful-One will close the door against those who ask for pardon!

If thou art wise, petition the Just-One; and the night of repentance will abridge the day of wrong-doing.

The Merciful-One, who brought thee, a non-entity, into being—is it wonderful that He, if thou be falling, should take thee by the hand!

If thou art a servant, lift-up the hand of supplication; and, if thou hast cause for shame, rain-down the waters of regret.

No one hath come to this door to implore forgiveness, whose transgression will not have been washed away by the torrent of repentance.

God will not wipe-out the character of him, whose fault hath been wiped out by his many tears.—*Graf's Text, p.* 430.   *Transl. II.* 123.

Sadi at the Grave of his Child.

Whilst I was at Senâa, I lost a child:—Why talk of the blow which then fell upon my head?

Fate never formed an image of comeliness like Joseph's, that a fish did not become like Jonah's its tomb.

In this garden no cypress ever reached its full stature, that the blast of destiny did not tear its trunk from the root.

It is not wonderful that roses should spring out of the earth, when so many rose-like forms sleep within its clay.

I said in my heart: "Die! for, shame to man, the child departeth unsullied, and the old man polluted!"

In my melancholy and distraction, whilst dwelling on his image, I erected a stone over the spot where he reposeth.

In terror of that place, so dark and narrow, my colour paled, and my senses failed me.

When from that disturbance my understanding came back to me, a voice from my darling child struck mine ear:

"If that dark spot make thee feel thy desolation, recall thy reason, and come out into the light.

Wouldest thou make the night of the tomb bright as day, light it up with the lamp of good works."

The body of the gardener trembleth as in a fever, lest the palm-tree should not produce its date.

Crowds are there of those who, greedy of the world's pleasures, think, that not having scattered the grain, they can yet gather in the crop;

But Sadi telleth you:—"Only he who planteth a tree will eat the fruit of it; only he who casteth the seed will reap the harvest."—*Graf's Text, p.* 431. *Transl. II.* 124.

FROM THE TENTH BOOK:
ON PRAYER.

Come, let us lift up our hands from the heart, for to-morrow it will not be possible to lift them up from the clay.

Dost thou not behold the tree in the winterly season, how it standeth leafless from the piercing cold!

See, how it holdeth out its hands in supplication, that, for pity's sake, it may not become empty-handed again;

That fate may restore to it its robe of honour; may replace in its lap its abundance of fruit!

Bethink thee of that door which is never closed, where the up-raised hand is never despairing!

Whither all may bring their devotion, and the wretched his supplication: and through which all may come to the court of the Comforter of the miserable!

Like the naked branch let us lift our hands; for we cannot sit longer before a leafless tree.

O Lord, do thou look down upon us benignantly, that our sins may be removed from thy servants whilst still in the body!

If thine earth-formed creatures commit faults, let it be in the hope of mercy from him who is the Pardoner of transgressors.

O Generous one, we have been nourished by Thy daily bread; Thy bounties and Thy grace have made our habit.

When the beggar beholdeth liberality, kindness, and soothing, let him not turn back from the track of the giver.

Since in this world thou hast regarded us as precious, let us keep in our eye that also which followeth it.

Greatness or meanness assign us, and it is enough! Great as Thou art, there is meanness from no one else!

Place not one like myself a ruler over my head; if I am to bear chastisement, it is better that it be from thee.

In the world, of bad there is nothing worse, than to bear injustice from one like oneself.

Shame in Thy face is enough for me ; let me not be ashamed in the sight of any other !

If a shadow from Thee fall upon my head, may my shield be Thy lowest step !

If Thou shouldest place a crown on my head and give me exaltation, do Thou uphold me, so that no one else shall cast me down!—*Graf's Text, p.* 433. *Transl. II.* 126.

Supplication.

My body still trembleth when I recall to memory the prayers of one absorbed in ecstacy in the Holy-place,

Who kept exclaiming to God with many lamentations :—"Cast me not off, for no one else will take me by the hand!

Call me to Thy mercy, or drive me from Thy door; on Thy threshold alone will I rest my head.

Thou knowest that we are helpless and miserable, sunk under the weight of low desires,

And that these rebellious desires rush on with so much impetuosity, that wisdom is unable to check the rein.

For they come on in the spirit and power of Satan, and how can the ant contend with an army of tigers!

Oh! lead me in the way of those who walk in Thy way, and from those enemies grant me Thy asylum!

By the essence of Thy majesty, O God; by Thine attributes without comparison or likeness;

By the—"Great is God"—of the pilgrim in the

Holy-house; by Him who is buried at Yathreb *(Medina)* on whom be peace *(Mohammed)* ;

By the shout of men of the sword *(great is God)*, who account their antagonists in the battle as women ;

By the devotion of the aged, tried, and approved ; by the purity of the young just arisen ;

In the whirlpool of the last breath, O save us in the last cry from the shame of apostacy *(denying Thy unity)* !

There is hope in those who have been obedient, that they may be allowed to make intercession for those who have not been obedient.

For the sake of the pure keep me far from contamination ; and if error escape me, hold me excused !

By the aged whose backs are bowed in obedience, whose eyes through shame for their past misdeeds look down upon their feet,

Grant that mine eye may not be blind to the face of happiness ; that my tongue may not be mute in bearing witness to the faith !

Grant that the lamp of truth may shine upon my path ; that my hand may be cut off from committing evil !

Cause mine eyes to be free from blindness ; withhold my hand from all that is unseemly.

A mere atom, carried about by the wind, O stay me in Thy favour !

Mean as I am, existence and non-existence in me are but one thing.

From the sun of Thy graciousness a single ray sufficeth me ; for except in Thy ray, no one would perceive me.

Look upon my evil, for on whomsoever Thou lookest, he is the better ; courtesy from a king is enough for the beggar.

If in Thy justice and mercy Thou receive me, shall I complain that the remission was not promised me?

O God, drive me not on account of my errors from Thy door, for even in imagination I can see no other door.

And if in my ignorance I became for some days a stranger to Thee, now that I am returned, shut not Thy door in my face.

What excuse shall I bring for the disgrace of my sensuality except to plead my weakness before the Rich-One.

Leave me not—the poor one—in my crimes and sins !—the rich man is pitiful to him who is poor.

Why weep over my feeble condition !—if I am feeble, I have Thee for my refuge.

O God, we have wasted our lives in carelessness!—
what can the struggling hand against the power of
fate!

What can we contrive with all our planning?—our
only prop is apology for our faults.

All that I have done Thou hast utterly shattered!—
what strength hath our self-will against the strength
of God!

My head I cannot withdraw from Thy sentence,
when once Thy sentence hath been passed on my head.
Graf's Text, p. 435. *Transl. II.* 127.

APPENDIX:

BEING AN EXTRACT FROM THE

MESNAVI, OF JELAL-UD-DIN-RUMI.

FROM THE MESNAVI OF JELAL-UD-DIN RUMI.

(Flourished in 13th Century.)

Divine Affections.

List how that reed is telling its story; how it is bewailing the pangs of separation!

Whilst they are cutting me away from the reed-bed, men and maidens are regretting my fluting.

My bosom is torn to pieces with the anguish of parting, in my efforts to express the yearnings of affection.

Every one who liveth banished from his own family, will long for the day which will see them re-united.

To every assembly I still bore my sorrow, whether the companion of the happy or the unhappy.

Every one personally was ever a friend, but no one sought to know the secrets within me.

My affections and my regrets were never far distant, but neither eye nor ear can always discern the light.

The body is not veiled from the soul, nor the soul

from the body, but to see the soul hath not been permitted.

It is love that with its fire inspireth the reed : it is love that with its fervour inflameth the wine.

Like the reed the wine is at once bane and antidote ; like the reed it longeth for companionship, and to breathe the same breath.

The reed it is that painteth in blood the story of the journey; and inspired the love-tale of the frenzied Mejnun.

Devoid of this sense we are but senseless ourselves ; and the ear and the tongue are but partners to one another.

In our grief our days glide on unprofitably ; and heart-compunctions accompany them on their way.

But if our days pass in blindness, and we are impure, oh ! remain Thou—Thou, like whom none is pure.

No untried man can understand the condition of him who hath been sifted : therefore, let your words be short, and let him go in peace.

Rise up, young man—burst thy bonds, and be free ! How long wilt thou be the slave of thy silver and thy gold ?

If thou shouldest fill thy pitcher from the ocean, what were thy store ?—The pittance of a day !

In the eye of the covetous man it would not be full. If the shell lay not contented in its bed, it would never be filled with the pearl.

He whose garment is rent by love divine—he only is cleansed from avarice and the multitude of sins.

Hail to thee, Love, our sweet insanity! O thou, the physician of all our ills!

Thou, our Plato and our Galen, the medicine of our pride and our self-estimation.

By love the earthly eye is raised to heaven, the hills begin to dance, and the mountains are quickened.

Could I join my lip to that of one who breatheth my breath, I would utter words as melodious as my reed.

When the rose garden is withered, and the rose is gone, thou wilt hear no longer news of the nightingale.

How should I be able any longer to retain my understanding, when the light of my beloved one no longer shineth upon me?

If the lover no longer receiveth his nourishment, he must perish like a bird deprived of its food.

A beloved one said to her lover—"O dear youth,
thou hast seen in thy travels many a city. Tell me,
then, which of them appeared to thee the most pleasant ?"

He replied —"That which contained her who robbed
me of my heart."

Wherever the sovereign of my soul spreadeth her
carpet of repose, that place, though it were the eye
of a needle, would seem boundless as the desert.

Wherever there is a maiden beautiful as Joseph
(*the Oriental type of perfect beauty*) and radiant as
the moon ; that place, though the bottom of a well,
would be an Eden.

With thee a prison would be a rose garden, O thou
ravisher of hearts : with thee Hell would be a Paradise,
O thou cheerer of souls.

The Merchant and the Parrot.

There was a merchant who possessed a parrot, a beautiful parrot, which he kept in a cage.

The merchant was preparing to make a journey, which he intended to begin with Hindustan ;

And the kind-hearted man called before him every man-servant and every maid-servant, and said,— "What present shall I bring for thee ? tell me frankly."

Each one of them answered him according to his desire; and to every one the good man promised what he asked.

Then he said to the parrot:—"And what present from the regions of Hindustan wilt thou have ?"

And the parrot answered : When thou see'st the parrots there, tell them my condition.

Say : " A certain parrot is yearning to see you, but is shut out by a cage from the free space of heaven.

He sendeth you his benediction, and asketh you to do him justice, and beggeth you to save his life, and to show him the paths of safety.

Is it right that I should consume my soul in vain longings, and that I should die here in loneliness?

Is it proper that I should be bound in hard shackles, whilst ye dwell amidst green places upon the trees?

Is this the kind of faith to keep with a friend? I in a cage and ye in a garden?

Call to mind, ye fortunate ones, that verdant lawn, and our morning draught in the midst of the meadows!

The remembrance of a friend should be a happy one to friends, as was that of Laila and Mejnun!

My comrades my precious idols, I am drinking cups of my own blood; drink ye to my remembrance one cup of wine, if ye desire to do me justice."

The merchant received the salutation and the message he was to carry to those of its race;

And when he reached the boundaries of Hindustan he saw in the desert a large company of parrots.

Then he staid his horse and lifted up his voice, and delivered the salutation and the message entrusted to him.

And immediately one of the parrots fluttered excessively, and fell down, and gave up its breath, and died.

Then the merchant repented him of what he had said and done, and exclaimed:—" Did I come to bring death to a living creature?

Perhaps this parrot was a relative of my parrot: perhaps they were two in body and one in soul.

Why did I do this?—Why deliver this message? My heart is on fire, and for this unlucky event I see no remedy.

The tongue is like flint, and the lip is like iron, and that which is struck in ignorance from the tongue is as flame.

Do not, foolish man, whether in easy good nature, or in idle boasting, strike flint and steel together!

For it is dark, and there is much cotton around, and in the midst of cotton wherefore scatter sparks!

A single word may desolate a world; can convert dead foxes into lions.

·————

When the merchant had finished his business he returned once more to his happy home.

For every man-servant he brought a present, and to every maiden he gave a token.

Then said the parrot:—" And what present hast thou brought to the captive?—Say! what hast thou seen, and what hast thou said?—Tell it me again."

He replied :—" Oh me! that of which I much repent ; that for which I could gnaw my hands and bite off my fingers.

" Wherefore did I foolishly carry that unlucky message, which I carried ignorantly."

It answered : " O merchant, repentance is of small value! what is it that requireth this passion and sorrow ?"

He replied : I delivered thy complaint to a company of parrots, thy fellows.

One of those parrots took such a share in thine affliction, that its heart broke, and it fluttered, and died."

When the parrot heard what that parrot had done, it too fluttered, and fell, and became cold. (*died*).

When he saw it fall in such wise, the merchant started-up, and dashed his cap upon the ground ;

And when he saw its colour and condition, he leaped-up, and tore the breast of his garment, and exclaimed :

" O my parrot, my beautiful, my dear one, what is this that hath befallen thee ?—Wherefore art thou thus ?

Alas! and alas! my bird of the melodious voice, who didst breathe the same breath, and knewest my every secret,

Alas! and alas! bird of the sweet notes, and tones of the harp; pleasant to me as my garden, and sweet as my sweet-basil!"

Then the merchant cast-out the dead bird from its cage, and immediately it flew up to a high branch of a tree.

He was amazed at the action of the bird, and was seized with desire to understand this strange mystery;

And turning his face upwards he said: "O my sweet one, to me sweet as a nightingale, give me, I pray thee, some explanation of what thou hast done."

It replied: "The message thou broughtest me gave me counsel. It said,—'Free thyself from speech and voice,

Since it was thy voice which brought thee into bondage;'—and it died itself to confirm the message."

The parrot then gave him one or two counsels, and bestowed upon him a parting benediction.

The merchant said to it:—"Depart in peace! thou hast shown me now a new path."

"Farewell! merchant," it replied, "thou hast done me a mercy; thy benevolence hath freed me from the chain and from the net."

Farewell! merchant; I WAS AWAY FROM MY HOME. May'st thou, by God's grace, become FREE LIKE ME.

NOTES AND ILLUSTRATIONS.

NOTE 1. PAGE 43.—" The Night of Power."

"Verily we sent down the Korân in the Night of Al Kadr (of power). And what shall make thee understand how excellent the Night of Al Kadr is? The Night of Al Kadr is better than a thousand months. Therein do the Angels descend, and the Spirit of Gabriel also, with the permission of their Lord, with his decrees concerning every matter. It is peace until the rising of the morn."—The Koran (*Sale's Transl.*), Surah 97.

NOTE 2. PAGE 51.—He turned fire into a bed of roses.

"And when Abraham was cast into the burning pile, we said,—O fire be cold, and a preservation unto Abraham."—Koran, Surah 21.

The legend referred to is, that Nimrod, to prevent Abraham from converting his people from their ancient gods, filled a large square with an immense quantity of wood, and had. Abraham cast into the blazing furnace, from which he was saved at the command of God by the angel Gabriel.

NOTE 3. PAGE 86.—"Put a saddle on a male lion." That is, by his devices and tricks control it as a horse; as we say, "can bell the cat."

"Abu Zaaid" (*misprinted Alu in the text,*) is the name of a Chess-player who had no equal, and was, moreover, a master in words and eloquence. The "Vizier"—the wise man, the councillor—is, but with more propriety than on our chess-board, our Queen. The "Horse" is our Knight.

The change of Vizier to Queen is due probably to the chivalric spirit of the times when chess was introduced from the East into Europe.

NOTE 4. PAGE 121.—"Thou may'st reach the Sidrah-tree itself:" or Paradise.

The Sidrah-tree is one of the trees in the Seventh Heaven; which is also the mansion of the angel Gabriel.

By the same Translator, and published in the same form, at 1s. 6d. each volume, by Williams & Norgate, Henrietta-street, Covent Garden, London; and James Cornish, Piccadilly, Manchester :—

www.ingramcontent.com/pod-product-compliance
Lightning Source LLC
Chambersburg PA
CBHW031059280326
41928CB00049B/1168